EXTRACTS

FROM THE

NARRATIVE OF MONS ANQUETIL DU PERRON'S TRAVELS IN INDIA

EXTRACTS

FROM THE

NARRATIVE OF MONS ANQUETIL DU PERRON'S TRAVELS IN INDIA

CHIEFLY THOSE

CONCERNING HIS RESEARCHES

IN THE

LIFE AND RELIGION OF ZOROASTER

TRANSLATER

KAVASJI EDALJI KANGA

GYAN

Published by

Gyan Publishing House
5, Ansari Road
Daryaganj, New Delhi-110002
Phone: 011-47034999, 9811692060
E-mail: books@gyanbooks.com

Distribution Network
gyanbooks.com
India, USA, Canada, UK, Australia

ISBN: 978-93-6780-400-1 (HB)

First Published, 1876

2nd Impression 2024

Printed at: Gyan Press, Delhi.

EXTRACTS FROM THE NARRATIVE OF
MONS ANQUETIL DU PERRON'S TRAVELS IN INDIA
Translater: KAVASJI EDALJI KANGA

EXTRACTS

FROM THE

NARRATIVE OF MONS. ANQUETIL DU PERRON'S TRAVELS IN INDIA,

CHIEFLY THOSE

CONCERNING HIS RESEARCHES

IN THE

LIFE AND RELIGION OF ZOROASTER,

AND IN THE

CEREMONIAL AND ETHICAL SYSTEM OF THE SAME RELIGION AS CONTAINED IN ZEND AND PEHLVI BOOKS,

TRANSLATED FROM THE FRENCH

BY

KAVASJI EDALJI KANGA,

TRANSLATOR OF THE VENDIDAD INTO GUJERATI, &c.

HEAD MASTER, MOOLLA FEEROZ MADRESA.

BOMBAY:

PRINTED AT THE "COMMERCIAL PRESS,"

BY DOSSABHOY EDULJEE.

1876.

PREFACE.

It may not be unknown to the reader that Mons. ANQUETIL DU PERRON was the first European scholar to come to India with the two-fold object of learning the religion of Zoroaster from the followers of the prophet themselves, and of acquainting the learned men of Europe in general, and those of his own country in particular, with the result of his studies. It is true that *previous* to his time Dr. Hyde had sought to create an interest in Zoroastrian lore by the publication of a learned work on it; and that *since* his time many eminent scholars have given to the world the results of their researches in the same direction. But from one point of view—and that an important one—to him alone belongs the credit of having been the first, as he seems to have been hitherto the last, European labourer in the field of Zoroastrian studies. He came to India with the express object of learning all about the religion and literature of the Parsis from their own lips, stayed there for several years, devoting them to the prosecution of this single purpose, and on his return carried with him to Europe a large and valuable collection of Zoroastrian manuscripts, depositing them with *la Bibliotheque du Roi* at Paris. Dr. Hyde, on the contrary, had never travelled to India in the pursuit of the same object, and had never seen a Zoroastrian in all his life. Professor of Latin and Arabic at Oxford he had no opportunities of learning Zend and Pehlvi, which Mons. Anquetil had during his sojourn among the Parsi Dustoors at Surat. And consequently his knowledge of the religion and literature of the Parsis was confined to a few small books written in Persian. Therefore, even though it was the accidental sight of a few pages of Dr. Hyde's publication which first kindled the spirit of enterprise in the bosom of the adventurous Frenchman, yet the debt due to him, compared with that due to Dr. Hyde, by the scholars of Europe in general and Zoroastrians in particular, is great beyond measure. For not only did he, by means of his published works, excite a warm interest in Zoroastrian literature among numerous scholars, but by his thoughtful act of depositing in a large public library the precious collection of Zoroastrian manuscripts he had carried with him from Surat, he rendered immense service to students of that literature. These manuscripts enabled the *savants* of the succeeding generations to study directly from the originals the sacred literature of the Parsis, and to throw, with the aid of a superior scientific learning, an amount of light on many a disputed and obscure question of Zoroastrian theology. All this debt of gratitude the Parsis have no means of discharging beyond an humble but unfeigned tribute of their admiration and praise.

Thanks, then, to his almost inspired devotion to the cause of Zoroastrian literature, his indefatigable exertions, his anxiety and foresight to preserve to posterity the fruits of his labours, reaped under perils and struggles which might have appalled any but a great enthusiast, his successors in the same path have availed themselves of his manuscripts, and illumined to a great extent the obscurity in which Zoroastrian lore was shrouded by lapse of ages. It has been with the study of Zend as it has been with the study of the inscriptions and architecture of the caves. Philological light has in the former, as magnesium light in the latter, illumined many dark places in the structure of Zend, and in the philosophy and ethics of Zoroaster. For this we are indebted to European scholars who have been and are the only expounders of the Zend Avesta. The deep researches of Burnouf, Westergaard, Spiegel, and Haug have given rise to a new school among the Parsis, which during the last 15 years has read and interpreted Zend and Pehlvi on the recognised principles laid down by these scholars, and of which Mr. K. R. Cama may deservedly be called the founder. Under his kindly auspices and fostering care it had made a considerable advance, when the arrival of the late lamented Dr. Haug in Bombay, in 1860, and his sojourn there for as many as seven years, gave it that additional impetus which was so highly requisite for the accomplishment of the great object, viz., a correct understanding of the Zend Avesta. The fruits of all this are now being reaped, but, it must be regretfully confessed, only to a slight extent. The Parsis ought by no means to remain contented with them such as they are. It were devoutly to be wished that they would have Anquetil for their great model, and snatch a spark from the fire of his enthusiasm and zeal. Let them picture to their mind the heroic French traveller of the past century, coming out to India with the determination of exploring the vast but little known fields of Oriental literature, under overwhelming physical and political difficulties, and without any of those facilities, conveniences and comforts which steam navigation, railways and telegraphs have made the generations of the last half a century familiar with under British rule. It would be highly desirable to have some adventurous souls from among us Parsis to emulate his daring enterprise and undertake travels, with aspirations equally noble and patriotic, to their ancestral land, and there to explore those remains which yet proclaim the religion of Zoroaster—remains which ought to be examined and interpreted ere the lords of the land complete their destruction, or the devouring tooth of time renders them valueless for all purposes of archæological investigations.

And here I trust to be pardoned a little digression. The reader will observe that whatever knowledge Anquetil derived was from Dustoor Darab, who belonged to the old school which was ignorant of Zend Grammar or the labours of modern philology. That science has enabled us to discover several errors into which Anquetil seems to have been led by the said teacher. These errors I have humbly attempted to point out in foot-notes in the translation. But I shall here refer to one of them which is important, and into which the French *savant* has fallen. Anquetil says that Zarvâna Akarana, *i. e.*, time without bounds—eternity—is the First Cause. He places Ahuramazda and Ahriman in the chain of secondary causes. This view is entirely incorrect, and all the European authorities on the subject are entirely opposed to it. I shall briefly state below how came this erroneous dogma to be at all accepted by Dustoor Darab, for, indeed, it would be wrong to accuse Anquetil of its invention. In that portion of the Zoroastrian scriptures, which, even when put to the severest test of criticism, maintains its reputation for genuineness and originality, as coming direct from Zoroaster himself, Ahuramazda is mentioned as the First Creative Cause. He is held to be the Supreme God, unequalled and without a rival. He existed before eternity, if that could be conceived. And as a proof thereof it is related that the Word, the creative fiat, Yathâ Ahû Vairyô, was spoken in eternity by Him. Ahuramazda employed two agencies, one creative and one destroying, to keep the world agoing. Each was indispensable to the other. Both are said to be creating in the wide sense, for the destroying was as much a creating agent, as without his help the creating agency would stand still. The world was not only destroyed in the natural cause by natural decay and decrepitude, but it was observed that moral and physical diseases, produced partly by nature, but mainly by the miscomprehension, negligence and discarding of the laws of nature by human beings, were also instrumental in bringing the world to a hasty and premature depravity, decay and death. These diseases were very naturally attributed to the natural destroying agency, to Ahriman. Thus an adventitious additional attribute was given to that agency which it had not at first. It was prominently noticed in relation to daily human life. Its original attribute was in time lost sight of in the presence of every day ever-recurring exemplification of his latterly conceived attribute. Ahuramazda being the Supreme God, the creative agency was in course of time generally identified with him, and men began to conceive two agencies at work, Ahuramazda for good and Ahriman for evil. These two being placed antagonistic to each other, the dogma of Dualism was prominently brought into conception. It was not forgotten, however, that Ahuramazda was the Supreme God, and it puzzled the later interpreters and commentators to explain how He the Supreme God could possibly have an antagonist. So the attributes themselves were unwarrantably made to represent *two* First Causes. Hence the dogma of Dualism. Later interpreters and commentators were more puzzled still to understand how He the Supreme God could possibly have an antagonist. Some one seems to have deluded himself into the belief that Zarvâna Akarana—eternity—was *above* even Ahuramazda and Ahriman. For a time this belief gained ground, and it was complacently thought that the religion was saved from the stigma of being condemned as dualistic. The disciples of this school taught that Zarvâna Akarana was *the* Original Cause, and Ahuramazda and Ahriman were his two agencies, the one creative and the other destroying. To this school Dustoor Darab seems to have belonged. The orthodox section of the Parsi community still believes in the two agencies as represented by Ahuramazda and Ahriman respectively, but they have no idea of Zarvâna Akarana being at their head. Thanks to the learned researches and impartial verdicts of Zend scholars in general, and the late lamented Dr. Haug in particular, the meshes into which the errors of one age after another had involved the original conception of the Supreme Deity have now been disentangled. It is now a proved and ascertained fact that Ahuramazda is the only One and Supreme God; Spentô mainyus and Angrô mainyus (Ahriman) are merely His two agents, the one creative and the other destroying; that all moral and physical diseases are attributed to the latter agency: hence Ahriman's agency is more known and widely felt, and dreaded as inimical to the welfare and happiness of men.

And now a word as to the following translation itself. Among the French Oriental works which I read some time since with the valued assistance of my esteemed tutor, Mr. K. R. Cama, was Mons. Anquetil du Perron's elaborate account of his Travels in India together with his essays on the Zoroastrian religion. I found it very interesting, and persuaded that some of the important extracts therefrom, chiefly those relating to his researches in the religion of Zoroaster and his *precis* of the ethics of the prophet,* would prove equally interesting to my co-religionists who may be unable to read the text in the original, I humbly attempted the task of translating them. By trying to adhere to too faithful a translation, I fear I have made myself obscure here and there, and have been betrayed in some places into inelegant English. I beg to be excused for these faults—unavoidable in a first attempt at translating from a highly idiomatic language into another equally so.

Of the chapters I have translated I would specially commend the third to the study of all young Zoroastrians. If not presumptuous, I would take the liberty of commending it also to the Heads of our Parsi schools, on whom has now devolved the duty of imparting religious instruction to the rising generation of Parsi youth under

---

* A portion of this essay was translated by the Rev. J. Murray Mitchell and published in the Journal of B. B. R. A. Society in 1845.

their charge. They will derive therefrom a fair and healthy conception of the whole fabric of Zoroastrianism.

In conclusion I cannot refrain from acknowledging that this translation would not have seen the light of day, but for the encouragement so cordially and uniformly accorded to it by our well-known Oriental scholar, Mr. K. R. Cama, to whom in this instance, as in many others, I owe a deep debt of gratitude.

Mr. Kanga, an intelligent and learned Mobed of the Parsi Community of Bombay, has translated from French into English the most interesting passages of the Narrative of Anquetil du Perron of his voyage to India, and the difficulties encountered by him in the acquisition and interpretation of the Zoroastrian manuscripts in the ancient Parsi languages, on which his great work is founded. The Mobed has executed his work with commendable accuracy and good taste; and on this account, I think him entitled to the patronage of the Parsi Community.

Malabar Hill, 7th August 1875.

JOHN WILSON, D. D.

This is to certify that the undersigned has compared a number of passages in Mr. Cowasji Edulji Kanga's manuscript translations from the work of M. Anquetil du Perron with the French text, and has found them faithfully rendered into English.

Khetvadi, 25th July 1875.

EDWARD REHATSEK.

EXTRACTS FROM THE

NARRATIVE OF MON. ANQUETIL DU PERRON'S TRAVELS IN INDIA,

CHIEFLY THOSE

RELATING TO HIS RESEARCHES ON THE RELIGION OF ZOROASTER.

The Religion and History of the Parsis are subjects, which, beyond being interesting in themselves, merit moreover the attention of *savants,* on account of the connection which this people had with the Hebrews, the Egyptians, the Greeks, the Indians, and even with the Chinese. But to trust solely to what the ancient writers tell us of that nation would be to run the risk of getting but an imperfect idea of it. The works which treat thoroughly of its History and Religion exist no more; and those that have escaped the ravages of time cannot give us a sure and satisfactory knowledge of it.

These reflexions induced the learned Dr. Hyde, at the end of the last century, to go deeply into a subject, which, up to then, had hardly been attended to. He perused the Arabian and Persian authors, added to these monuments the testimony of travellers and the letters which many of his friends had written to him from India, and wrote his famous work on the Religion of the Parsis.

This book can be taken to be the only one, which gives a series of instructive details, extracted from Oriental works about the Parsis. Unfortunately, the principal sources, from which Dr. Hyde had drawn them, are not of the first antiquity. The English doctor cites particularly the Farhang-e Jehangiri, a Persian Dictionary, commenced in the 16th century in the reign of Shah Akbar and completed in the 17th century, in that of Jehanghir, and quotes several passages from the Viráf Námeh and Sadder—works, long posterior to Zoroaster, of which he possessed only the translations made in modern Persian. But as this doctor knew neither Zend nor Pehlvi,* we do not find in his work any passage from the Yaçna or from the Niâyesh, which naturally formed part of his Mss. He contents himself with mentioning the *Zend Avesta*, without translating any passages from it. With the English, his work could therefore only pass for a mere essay.

The surest way was to consult the Parsis themselves on their religion; and there was nothing of impossibility in the enterprise. Gujerat, in India, where they settled more than 900 years ago, offers a great number of their body. They are, moreover, scattered to the north of the Malabar Coast, where the love of commerce and industry, which characterise them, has procured them considerable establishments. They are called in India *Parsis* or *Parses*; I shall, in the following pages, make use of this last name to designate this precious remnant of the disciples of Zoroaster.

It was from the hands of the Parsis settled at Surat, that George Bourchier, an Englishman, received in 1718 the Vendidad Sádé. This volume which contains three Zend

---

* This point has been convincingly proved by the learned Frenchman at the end of his first volume.—*Translator.*

works, viz., the Vendidad properly so called, the Yaçna and the Vispered, was only brought into England in 1723. It appeared in Europe for the first time, and no one could then decipher its characters, although the Zend Alphabet existed in one of the Mss. of Dr. Hyde. Long after, a Councillor of Bombay, Mr. Frazer, a Scotchman, known by the life which he had given of Tamaskoulikhan, went to Surat in search of the works of Zoroaster, which he thought he would be able to collect at that place. He succeeded in his efforts with regard to the purchase of two Zend books, viz., the Yaçna and the Yashts, and several other Persian and Indian Mss.; but it was impossible for him to induce the priests to teach him either Zend or Pehlvi, and to give him the key to the Zend-Avesta. Little satisfied with his voyage, he returned to England where he died soon after.

Such were the attempts which the English made for the acquisition and the understanding of the works attributed to Zoroaster. The rest of Europe trusted to Dr. Hyde, without thinking of learning the languages of which the *savants* knew hardly the names. This general supineness for an object so interesting astonished me, and I conceived from that time the idea of the voyage which I made to India.

In 1754, I had an occasion to see at Paris four Zend leaves copied from the Vendidad Sádé, which is at Oxford. Immediately I resolved to enrich my mother country with this singular work. I ventured to entertain the idea of translating it, and of going with that view to Gujerat or Kirman to learn the ancient Persian. This work could expand the ideas which I had formed on the origin of languages, and on the changes which they are subject to. It was moreover very proper to throw light on the Antiquity of the Orientals, which one would vainly search for among the Greeks or the Latins.

I thought then that, I had no other means to succeed than to go to and acquire from the Parsis themselves the knowledge which I was in need of, instead of trusting to conjectures, by following in the footsteps of the English *savant* (Dr. Hyde). Moreover, I knew that the four Vedas (the sacred books of the Hindoos) were written in ancient Sanscrit, and that *la Bibliotheque du Roi* was rich in Indian Mss., which no person understood. These reasons induced me to prefer India to Kirman, more especially as I could there dive equally deep into ancient Persian and ancient Sanscrit.

I communicated my project to M. l'Abbé Sallier, to M. l'Abbé Barthelemy, to M. le Comte de Caylus, to Messieurs Falconner, de Bougainville and de Guignes. These *savants* approved of it. They pointed out to me from a distance *l'Academie des Belles-Lettres* as the goal of my labours; they also promised to talk to the minister on my behalf and to induce *la Compagnie des Indes* to countenance my views. I had consequently the honor of conversing several times on this subject with M. de Silhouette, Royal Commissioner to *la Compagnie des Indes;* and the manner in which he listened to me showed him as much a man of letters as a patron of incipient talents.

But the impatience to commence a career, which I foresaw ought to be long and sown with difficulties, did not permit me to expect that the promises of persons, who interested themselves in the execution of my plan, would be realised. I had, moreover, resolved, in order that I might not be exposed to reproaches in case of ill success to depend on myself alone in an enterprise of this nature; and justice did not allow that I should exact from my family, little favored as it was with the blessings of fortune, the assistance which could appear more than precarious.

Under these circumstances, confident in the strength of my constitution, and inured as I was for many years to an austere life, to night studies and sobriety, the calling of a soldier to *la Compagnie des Indes* appeared to me to be the only one which the state of things permitted me to embrace. I went consequently to see M. Boucher, the officer charged with the enlistment of recruits for India, and after some moments of conversation on the history of the country and on the affairs of the Coromandel Coast, I declared to him openly the object of my visit. My proposal surprised him; he strongly represented me, but with a sort of tenderness, the difficulty in which I should be involving myself, and deferred me for four days, thinking this delay would make me change my resolution. It is difficult to express what passed within myself during this interval. I went again at the end of four days to see M. Boucher; my courage triumphed over his objections: and seeing that I was firm, he accepted my enlistment with a positive promise to speak of it only after my departure.

I employed the little time which preceded it in preparing, without the knowledge of my parents, my small equipment, which consisted of two shirts, two handkerchiefs and a pair of stockings. I swelled my packet with a box of mathematical instruments, and with the Hebrew Bible of Leusden, of Montagne, of Charron; and the day before my departure from Paris, I sent for my brother who is at present Chief of the French Factory at Surat. What an interview! I cannot think of it without shuddering. The note which I had written to him informed him of the business in two words. I wanted more than human fortitude to get over his chagrin and mine. M. Boucher left me in his presence master of my fate. We stared at each other's face. His tears were his expressions; mine suffocated me. With that strength which a cool and thoughtful temper gives, I proved to him that the resolution I had formed was needful. He promised to keep my secret for two days, and after having received from him some presents, I had yet the strength to leave him first to rejoin the troops with which I was to go to the East. The moment for departure having arrived, I distributed among my new comrades the outfits which *la Compagnie des Indes* had given to their soldiers; and we began to march on foot, commanded by an inferior officer of the Invalids, on the 7th November 1754, before day-break, to the lugubrious sound of a badly mounted drum.

The road from Paris to the East was for me an apprenticeship of fatigues, which I underwent with more firmness than I could have dared expect. The journey was of ten days, partly on foot and partly on horseback, in the midst of rains, cold, snow and accompanied with dangers of more than one kind. Frequently, I found myself obliged to carry my portmanteau for several leagues through cultivated fields, to go to enjoy some hours of repose in a poor hut, where I could hardly, even on payment, find the necessaries of a recruit. What occupied me usefully, and even in some way, agreeably during this laborious march were the new characters, whose different shades my situation enabled me to observe.

I arrived at the East on the 16th November. M. Godehen d'Igoville, Director of the Company, had been informed of my object by M. Falconet, his friend. When somebody went and told him that there was a soldier the Company who wished to talk to him, he said, coming out hastily from the room, certainly he must be M. Anquetil. "Is it possible," addressing me, "that you have formed such a resolution?" At the same time he wrote to the Major of the troops to conduct me to the town, leaving me at liberty to lodge at any place where I wished, and to take what measures I found proper for the arrangement of my affairs.

The next month he freed me from my enlistment by order of the minister, and informed me that the King had accorded me a pension of five hundred francs. This was a series of good services by M. l'Abbé Barthelemy, whose friends, M. le Comte de Caylus, M. Bignon and M. Lamoignon de Malesherbes had talked in my behalf to M. de Silhouette and to M. le Contrôleur Général. On the very day of my departure, my enlistment had been carried to the office of the Company; M. Saint-Ard, Director, being informed by my kinsmen, had withdrawn it; and immediately after, my friends had worked to procure me a means of living suitable to my plan, for the execution of which I had in some measure forced the events.

On their part *la Compagnie des Indes* gave me a free passage on board one of their vessels, *le Duc d'Aquitaine,* the table of the captain and a cabin; and I got ready to part for the East Indies with a resolution to bring home thence the laws of Zoroaster and those of the Brahmins. I was at Port-Louis, when a gun, fired at 7 in the morning, 24th February 1755, gave me notice that I should go on board the ship.

* * * * *

I arrived at Pondichery on the 10th of August 1755. Seeing that modern Persian was the language most extensively used in Asia, and spoken in all the places where the difference of idioms or rather of dialects rendered the knowledge of Malabari of that part insufficient, I made it the object of my study without neglecting the last. The teacher I took up for Persian knew neither French nor Portuguese. The first lessons were learnt by signs; I pointed out to him various objects; then I wrote down their names as he gave them; I repeated these names. In this manner I learned a jargon, which, in three months, made me understand it, though sufficiently badly. As for my teacher he learned not from me twenty words of French.

My object, after having made myself familiar with Persian, was to go into the interior to acquaint myself with the Malabarese language, to visit the Brahmins and learn Sanscrit near some celebrated Pagoda. But after a mature consideration I hastened the execution of this plan.

I arrived at Chandanagore on Maundy-Thursday, 22nd April 1756, weakened by fever. I wished, however, during the intervals of my illness to put my affairs in some order: I went consequently to see the Director and requested him to settle my salary. My representations were useless. I reiterated them many a time and the Director told me plainly that he had not the letters of M. de Leyrit who had written to him about me. As regards the interpreters of the Company whom I begged to engage to assist me in my project, his answer was that they were not allowed to serve private individuals. So I was obliged to apply to my friends to get a Moor who would speak Persian with me, and to live for two months at their expense. I thought it necessary to inform M. de Leyrit of the conduct of the Superintendent of Chandanagore towards me. At last, whether the latter had received some new orders or whether my demands had appeared to him more just, he ordered my salary to be paid at what I used to get at Pondichery. My youth, the little reality which my projects represented, and the conduct of some private person, who, almost under the same pretext, had wasted, they said, 20 to 30 thousand Rupees of the Company—these were likely the causes of the difficulties, which I had experienced from the Director of the Company.

These proceedings absolutely disgusted me with the Colony of Chandanagore; I did not acquire any particular knowledge there. I hardly went to one or two families, but passed my time in translating some Persian books, in promenading in the outskirts of the town which were charming, and in conversing with the Bengalees. I went, especially, to the Pagodas and to the houses of artisans; I examined their tools and wrote down their names.

At last to neglect no means either near or distant, tending to the execution of my plan, I sent to M. Le Verrier, Chief of the French Factory at Surat, two lines written in Zend characters, accompanied with the translation which I had made. * * * * *

I was confined to bed with fever and dysentery for three months and was reduced to the last extremity. I was expected every moment to breathe my last; delirium and death-rattle announced within me approaching dissolution. Several persons even carried to the Coast the news of my death, by a vessel which set sail at that time. In this state of prostration, I discharged some worms, and the dysentery ceased. By degrees, I was able to take some spoonsful of soup. My strength recovered, and in less than twenty days, I was in a state to leave my room.

Soon, the complete return of my strength made me feel the uselessness of the life I led. Bengal was then in combustion; the Nabob had driven out the English from their establishments, and this revolution foreboded in this province a future of troubles, which could only interfere with some purely literary operations of mine. I resolved to leave Chandanagore, but was uncertain whither to take my steps. In the mean time, a letter, which I received from Surat, fixed my destination. It was the answer of M. Le Verrier, who informed me that the Parsis had read the lines which I had sent to him; that they were written in modern Persian, but in Zend characters. He added that their Dustoors had showed him the works of Zoroaster, and particularly, the Zend and Pehlvi Vendidad, and that they had promised to explain that work to me and to teach me their ancient languages. This news restored me to all my former health, and my departure was resolved upon. I embarked my luggage on board a vessel which was to have descended the Ganges; but the news of war between France and England compelled her to return and disconcert my project.

What a situation! the works of Zoroaster exist; his followers are ready to give and explain them to me; I was separated from that treasure which I held of great value to enrich my native country; and it came to this that I allowed it to slip for ever, and that without any consideration from the Chief, without any other resource but my badly paid salaries, I followed the fate of a caravan, brave as it was no doubt, still in danger of falling under the steel of the English, if they should attack it; exposed thereby to be led as a prisoner to Europe, at the very moment when I was about to reach the goal of my travels! I felt this blow but concealed it.

* * * * *

I arrived at last at the port of Surat on the 1st of May 1758, at 5 o'clock in the evening, extremely weakened by dysentery. It was necessary to wait for some time for a passport from the Nabob: afterwards a peon of the French Consul came to take me; and within half an hour I had the pleasure to embrace my brother at the French Residency.

Before entering into the details of what passed at Surat during the three years that I remained there, I think it proper to say something about the origin of this town. Though it has suffered much by the invasion of the Moors (Mahomedans) and the Marathas, and has been several times pillaged, Surat is one of the largest and most populated towns of India. Originally, it was only a collection of huts belonging to fishermen, who used to muster together on the southern bank of the Tapti. It was not known even in the thirteenth century, though Cambay was then already celebrated. Here is what Nourbeg, librarian of the last Mahomedan Soubedar of Ahmedabad, tells me about the origin of this town.

In the reign of Mahmoud Begadâ, fifth king of Ahmedabad, who flourished about the close of the fifteenth century, there were (in the vicinity of a place where in 1760 stood the house of Fares Khan, second of the town), several huts of fish-mongers, who had at their head a man of their profession, named Suratji. This chief paid the dues for his little village to the Hâkem (i. e. to the governor) of Rânder (a small town situate on the northern bank of the Tapti), who ruled the country on behalf of the king of Ahmedabad. The Portuguese, in their incursions, having plundered the banks of that river, Suratji, whose people were without any means of defence, and who had suffered considerably, carried his complaints to the king of Ahmedabad. This prince, having inquired what the land of these fishermen could produce, ordered Khodavand Khan, Governor of Rânder, to erect a fortress, which might place the town of Suratji under shelter from every insult. Khodavand Khan at first chose the site on the place where there now is his tomb, near the house of Fares Khan and that of Fakir Kheirulla; but as it was at some distance from the river, the choice of it was abandoned. He then pitched upon another site near Bâgh Talâo, where there now are Shroffs (bankers) about half a coss* from the river. This was also abandoned for the same reason, it being found difficult to carry water from the river to that distance, in order to fill up the ditches with which he intended to surround the fortress. At last its foundations were laid in the place where it now stands; and Khodavand Khan promised Suratji to give the latter's name to this city, as a reward for the site which he ceded to him (Khodavand Khan). This city was then called Surat after Suratji. The inscription, which I have cited in the note,† informs us that the fortress was completed only in 931 Hijree (1524 A. C.) The town rose with the times; in 1666 it had yet only some walls of earth in very bad state. The first *enceinte* was constructed some years after, and the se-

---

* A coss is a measure of distance about two miles in length.—*Translator.*

† *Sadd bu-ved bar sina-i jân-e Ferangi in benâ (Pers.)* = this fortress is built to check the progress of the Ferangees (the Europeans).

cond some more than fifty years ago, under the Nabobship of Hyder Kouli Khan: each has 12 gates, and is adorned with round towers where some guns are to be seen.

I now recur to the course of my travels. Arrived at Surat, I went to the French Residency where my brother expected me. Every help, which I was in need of, was given to me there; and some days of repose restored me sufficiently from the fatigues which I had endured. I still felt however some symptoms of dysentery, which the change of food had produced. Seeing my illness increased, notwithstanding the strength of my constitution, and wearied of the remedies and the visits of a European, who styled himself a physician, I gave myself up to an unrestricted diet; and by taking several doses of ipecacuanha which I had brought with me from Mahi, I cured myself of the complaint in about a month and a half.

The kind of life I led after my convalescence contributed not a little to the re-establishment of my health, which required a strict regimen. Many reasons had induced me to take a private lodging and to appear rarely at the French Factory. The peevish, sarcastic and exacting nature of the French Consul always found something or other to quarrel for. These were the difficulties, especially, continued delay and remissness which would allow no business which could be done immediately to be finished. After a good many communications, I saw the Parsi Dustoors, for whom I had made the voyage to Surat, and from whom I had to learn the religion of Zoroaster. They were Dustoors Darab and Kaous, High Priests of one of the two sections into which the Parsis of Surat are divided. In the first instance, there was the difficulty about the manuscript which, they asserted, had been received from their Legislator.

They engaged to copy it out for me for Rs. 100: this involved some time; and being desirous to make up for the years which I thought I had lost, I commenced without delay the study of their ancient languages. From that time forward, I got a notion of the conduct of the people at the French Factory. They attempted to keep up their importance, and feared lest I should too early engage myself in this matter. I resolved to dispense with their aid and conduct my affairs myself. For this purpose I was obliged to leave the French Residency, where I was in difficulties, and where I already found myself greatly inconvenienced.

I felt these unfavorable circumstances less than the conduct of my Dustoors; I despaired of their tardiness. After a stay of three months in Surat, I received at last the promised manuscript. This was the Vendidad, the twentieth work of their Legislator, a quarto volume, written in Zend and Pehlvi. I did not discover till some time after that it was mutilated and incorrect, and after having paid them its price, I thought to begin immediately the study of this work. But the Dustoors, fearing to see me quick at my studies, wished that I should commence with the alphabet. I wrote down what they dictated to me. This enabled me to decipher the characters in which the Vendidad was written.

These first steps did not please my Dustoors, who believed I was nearly escaping from their hands: their answers to my questions were more reserved. They affected a mysterious tone, believing it gave importance to their lectures. Long absence, under the pretext of the dangers they were exposed to by coming to my place, intervened between their visits. Once they talked to me of the offer of a considerable sum of money which Mr. Fraser had made to them for obtaining some Pehlvi manuscripts, and of the remuneration which was reserved in England for any one, who would translate their sacred books.

As long as M. Le Verrier remained at Surat, it was not possible for me to obtain anything from the Parsi Dustoors, except the Zend and Pehlvi Vendidad and some general explanations on their religion. To have demanded of them to keep their word would have been labour lost: perceiving also the little importance which the French Consul attached to me, they imperceptibly retired.

I was then in a very sorry plight, and exposed to the same treatment which I had experienced in Bengal. They denied me the privilege of visiting the French Residency with a hatred, which had the effect of separating me from the natives. I was obliged to make formal applications to the French Consul, and to complain bitterly of his proceedings to the superior council and to the Governor of Pondichery; to send to the latter copies of the letters, which I had received from M. le Comte de Caylus, and from M. Boutin, Royal Commissioner to the French East India Company, recommending me to the governor, and authorising him to advance me some money. Whilst waiting for a reply to this request, I was not in a position to repay what I had borrowed at Goa in order to go to Surat. I was obliged to reduce myself to a repast of lentils and rice called by natives *Khichri*, so that I might be able to spare from my income something to discharge a part of my debts, and to buy the books which I was in need of, and with all that to work also.

What could have been the reasons of this whimsical and harsh conduct of M. Le Verrier, otherwise a man of sense and probity and even religious? They were probably the rarity of my visits, my carelessness in making my respects, the distance which I always kept from the spirit of partisanship, and no doubt the silence of the Governor of Pondichery, who had not introduced me at Surat in the manner I had been flattered he would. I draw a veil over these inconsistencies, which show the feebleness of humanity. Perhaps the reader will not pardon me for having inflicted this upon him. But I only bring to mind, with a sort of compassion, these grievous and frequently prolonged reflections during all the night, about the difficult position in which I was, after having come from the interior of Bengal, to search and translate at Surat the books of Zoroaster.

In the midst of these difficulties, which I may call private, I pulled on sufficiently well with the members of the European communities settled at Surat, and especially with the Chief of the Dutch Factory, M. Taillefer, a gentleman of letters and politeness. As Mancherji, his broker, was the head of the Parsi community at Surat, I thought that he or his Dustoor must have a copy of the manuscript, which the Dustoors of M. Le Verrier had copied for me. Besides, as he was a personal enemy of my Dustoors, a comparison of his manuscript with theirs would test the authenticity of the copy of Dustoor Darab: that was the means of discovering the truth rather than the relation subsisting between the two parties. My hopes were not futile: M. Taillefer, at the end of November, sent me the Zend and Pehlvi Vendidad of Mancherji, giving me to understand that this Parsi had assured him, that it was the most authentic and most correct copy which could be had at Surat. At the same time he prayed me to take care that no pages were lost, and to return it as soon as possible.

As soon as I found myself in possession of this treasure,

I compared it word by word with my copy; and finding a considerable difference between the two, I wrote back to M. Taillefer, praying him to induce Mancherji to leave me his manuscript for some time more. My object was to note from them, as I have done, the differences.

The answer (to this my request) from the head of the Dutch Factory (M. Taillefer) was very polite: without granting me positively what I required, he promised to talk about this matter to his agent. As for me, resolved to profit by the occasion, I commenced my work. I wished that my Dustoors had aided me in my revision: but I feared that if I should speak to them of it, the shame of finding themselves baffled might make them divulge the service which Mancherji had rendered to me; which, had it been done, would have induced that Parsi (Mancherji) to have asked for his book, before I had extracted from it that part which I wanted. Besides, seeing me short of money, they rendered themselves scarce. They hardly appeared once a fortnight.

At last, understanding how to reconcile these differences which I had discovered in the two manuscripts, which were given to me as being the same, I softly questioned my Parsi teachers. It was also with this view, that I had paid them handsomely for some Persian works which they wanted to get rid of. I also induced them to bring me a small Pehlvi and Persian Dictionary, which they had promised me; but the pretexts invented on the occasion prevented the promise being fulfilled.

M. Le Verrier left Surat in the beginning of January 1759, and the French Factory in this city (Surat) to my brother, who after some time received charge of its management.

Towards the commencement of February, seeing my business languish, I told Dustoor Kaous that his manuscript differed from the other Vendidads (that is, other copies of the Vendidad) of Gujerat, and showed him immediately the one belonging to Mancherji. He grew pale at the opening of the book, and at first feigned not to know this work, adding that it was some other book: he wished afterwards to maintain the authenticity of his copy (for he knew not that I had had the patience to compare the two manuscripts, word by word), and went away in a very bad humour. The next day, Darab, his father, who was more clever and more sincere, and who saw besides that I could no longer be deceived, brought me a copy perfectly similar to that of Mancherji, assuring me, that all the copies of the Vendidad resembled that which he had presented to me; and that the copy, which he had given me at first, was corrected in the Pehlvi translation; but that in the one in Zend, there were only a few transpositions and changes of letters of little importance. He promised, at the same time, to bring me a copy similar to that of Mancherji, and also an entirely Zend copy without the Pehlvi translation. These advances were accompanied by a Pehlvi and Persian Vocabulary, of which I have already spoken above, and some other manuscripts, some in modern Persian and some in ancient Persian (Zend and Pehlvi); and a small history in verse of the emigration of the Persians to India.

This history leads us to the history of the present Parsis, and makes us acquainted with the remaining disciples of Zoroaster, who have been the chief object of my researches at Surat. I think it would not be out of place to give an abridged account of it here.

It is known that Yezdegird, the last Persian king of

the Sassanian dynasty, was dethroned by Khalif Hazret Omar Ketab and died in 651 A. D. It is from the first year of the reign of this king (that is, from 632 A. D.), that the era of the Parsis begins.

The religion of Zoroaster then ceased to be dominant in Persia. Some months after the death of Yezdegird, the Parsis, persecuted by the Mahomedans, retired to Kohestán, where they remained one hundred years. Afterwards, they came down to Ormaz on the Persian Gulf; and after having settled fifteen years in that place, they set sail for India and landed at Div.*

The Parsis, and almost all the Oriental nations consult astrological books on important affairs. At first they throw the dice, then make a reference to the books of divination, which they call Fals, for the number indicated by the dice, and act according to the purport contained in that passage of the Fal, which corresponds to the number. The Parsis, at the end of nineteen years, believing what they found in their Fal that the sojourn at Div was not propitious to them, re-embarked on board ship; and after encountering a violent tempest, landed in a pleasant and fertile place, situated about three coss south of Nargor, which is seven coss from Daman on the way to Bassein.

When they landed ashore, one of their chiefs went to salute Jâdirah, an Indian Prince of that part of Gujerat, and made him some presents. The Rájá received them very warmly, but, seeing afterwards that these foreigners were numerous and well-armed, was apprehensive lest they

---

* A small Portuguese possession, situated to the north-west of Bombay.—*Translator*.

should give some trouble to his dominions: this induced him to propose to them five conditions capable, as he believed, to deter them from the design, which they had formed of establishing themselves in his country. The first condition was that they should disclose to him the mysteries of their religion; the second, that they should lay aside their arms; the third, that they should speak the Indian language; the fourth, that their females should appear in public without any veils on their face* like Indian females; the fifth and last, that they should celebrate their marriages in the evening according to the usage of the country.

As these five articles contained nothing contrary to the spirit of the Zoroastrian religion, the Parsis subscribed to them, and laid before the Rájá a *precis* of their religion. "Do not fear us," they said to him, "we are friends to all "Indians. We worship God; and the love of our religion "makes us flee from evil agents; we have abandoned every "thing for it (i. e. the religion). Descended from King "Jamsheed, we adore God and all that he has created. "We honor the sun, the moon and fire. We gird round "our waist the Koshti, which is composed of 72 threads. "We maintain that females who are in their monthly course "or in child-bed ought to be kept apart from other per-"sons." The Rájá, satisfied with this explanation, which was also set forth in the religion of the Hindoos, permitted the Parsis to take possession of any piece of ground which suited them; and these (the Parsis), approving of the choice made by their chiefs, built in the place thus accorded to them a town which they called Sanjân.

Some time after their peaceful settlement, the chief of

* So far as the translator knows, no such custom prevailed among the ancient Parsis.

the Dustoors reminded the Parsis of the vow they had made to erect in their new colony a great Fire-temple (Atash-Behrám), if they were saved from the tempest which had overtaken them at sea while starting from Div. They all consented to do so : consequently, the Dustoors went to the Rájá asking for a piece of land three farsangs* all round, so that the voice of the profane might not be heard in the sanctuary. The Rájá complied with their request; and the Parsis, full of zeal, contributed, with all their might, to make their new settlement flourish.

Three hundred years, more or less after Yezdegird, passed without any remarkable events, after which the Parsis separated. Some went to settle at Bankanir (9 or 10 coss from Bansdah); others in Broach (12 leagues to the north of Surat); some in Unklesur (between Surat and Broach); while others in Cambay (16 leagues to the north of Broach); many in Bariao, a village at the distance then of a small coss from the place, where there is the fortress of Surat, and which now forms in the north one of the suburbs of that city (Surat); others at last to Nowsaree (10 coss to the south of Surat.)

The two centuries which followed this dispersion presented nothing of any importance. In course of time Sanjân became depopulated ; the Dustoors disappeared ; Khoshest (Khorshed ?), a young Mobed and his son were the only true observers of their religion, of whom history makes mention up to 700 years after Yezdegird.

It was more than 500 years that the Parsis had settled in India, when the Mahomedans (for the first time)

---

* A farsang is a measure of distance, equal to about three miles. —*Translator.*

made their appearance at Chapanir (eight coss on that side of Cambay on the way to Ahmedabad). The name of the Rájá of Sanjân was well-known all over the country. Sultan Mahmoud (Mahomed Sháh), at that time being on the throne of Gujerat, wished to render this prince tributary and ordered Alaf Khan, his prime minister, to march against him. Alaf Khan soon set out with 60,000 horse. The Rájá, seized with fear at the view of the storm which menaced him, sent for the Parsi Dustoors, reminded them of the favours which he had heaped on them as well as on their ancestors, and thus induced them to assist him in this fray.

A review being held, 1,400 Parsis were found capable of bearing arms; they by a solemn promise devoted their lives to the Rájá. The first action was bloody. On one side the Parsis fought for life and liberty, on the other, the Mahomedans for glory. The Hindoos fell under the sword of the Mahomedans. Then Ardeshir, one of the chiefs of the Parsis, proposed to his brethren to fight in a body against the enemy. The Parsis, animated by his example, presented themselves in good order and spread terror in the army of Alaf Khan. They lost only one of their chiefs, named Kaous, who was killed by being stabbed with a spear. The camp, the tents and the baggage of the Mahomedans became the prey of the victorious Parsis.

The defeat was, however, not so general as to disable Alaf Khan from promptly raising a new army and collecting the remains of the first. Some days after he appeared at the head of a formidable *corps* of the Mahomedans. Though enfeebled by the preceding actions, the Rájá refused not the combat. The two armies stood face to face. Ardeshir, who saw the superiority of the army of Alaf Khan, demanded of the Rájá permission to go personally to confront the enemy, and went forth immediately equipped with all kinds of arms and a noose hanging from the saddle of his horse.

At the words of contempt which accompanied Ardeshir's defiance, a hero of Alaf Khan's army came forth. The two warriors, like tigers thirsty for blood, rushed at each other: but the valour of Ardeshir decided the victory; he dismounted his adversary, and after girding him with a snare, cut off his head. Alaf Khan, furious at seeing his hero vanquished, swore the destruction, both of the Parsis and of the Rájá. Immediately the two armies began to fight; the carnage on both sides was dreadful; Ardeshir, the bulwark of the Parsis, fell pierced with an arrow; many distinguished chiefs and the Rájá himself fell on the field of battle. The death of this prince terminated the fight. Sanjân was given up to pillage and reduced to Mahomedan subjection.

The Parsis, being obliged to quit Sanjân, took refuge in the mountains of Bahrout (near Chapanir), where they passed 12 years. They retired afterwards to Bansdah, a town situated 8 or 10 coss on this side of Aurangabad, carrying with them the Atash-Behrám. Their former friends went before them to receive them with great pomp. In a short time there was a general concourse at Bansdah. The Parsis of the surrounding places came to worship the Atash-Behrám; this kindled fresh zeal in their hearts.

It was about this time that Dustoor Ardeshir arrived in Gujerat from Sistan. He gave the Parsis a copy of the Vendidad with its Pehlvi translation. As the copy which the Parsis had brought with them to India was lost, two copies were made from Ardeshir's Vendidad; and it is from these two copies, that other copies of the Zend and Pehlvi Vendidad of Gujerat have been made.

Fourteen years passed without any important event. There appeared afterwards at Nowsaree a rich Parsi named Changâh Sháh, a faithful observer of the Zoroastrian law. He distributed his wealth among the poor, provided the Parsis with Koshtis and Sudras, and endeavoured to bring back those whom ignorance and troubles had led into many errors to the exact practice of the Zoroastrian law. To succeed in this, he applied to the Dustoors of Kirmán, consulting them on different points of the Zoroastrian religion, neglected in Gujerat. In course of time when something doubtful presented itself, the Dustoors of India, following the example of Changâh Sháh, wrote to those of Irán, and the answers of the latter form the works which are known by the name of Ravâets, that is, *histories, traditions, reports.*

Changâh Sháh represented to his fellow-citizens, that it was difficult to go to adore the Atash-Behrám at Bansdah, for the feast connected with its worship came on the 9th day of the month Ader, which was the time of the rainy season. He afterwards made them alive to the benefit of having the Atash-Behrám in their town and induced them to bring it there. The people applauded his proposal, and the Atash-Behrám was brought with great pomp from Bansdah to Nowsaree in the year 785 of Yezdegird (of Jesus 1415). The three Mobeds of Sanjân, who accompanied it, were charged to keep a watch over it in their turn with other Mobeds.

Here is the end of this small poetical work, which contains the history of the retreat of the Parsis in India. What I have said of the Vendidad brought by Ardeshir, of the letters written by Changâh Sháh to the Dustoors of

Kirman, and what I am now going to report about the quarrels which arose among the Parsis of India—these I have got from the Parsi Dustoors with whom I had conversed.

* * * * *

In order not to frighten away Darab, who thought to detain me one year at the Zend alphabet, I begged him to show me rare and valuable Zend works, with a promise to buy two Persian Mss. which he wanted to get rid of. When I was master of these books, I threatened to abandon him and Kaous (his father) to Mancherji,* their chief enemy, if he refused to aid me in translating the Vendidad in modern Persian. The stratagem succeeded: however, when he saw me write to his dictation, and question him about everything and hear him only with wrapt attention, fear seized him, for he felt that I was going to know thoroughly the dogmas of his religion. I was more than a month without seeing him back. He pretended that his death was certain, if the other Dustoors knew what he did at my place. Kaous maintained that I required information which their conscience would not permit them to give, and for which they were not bound. But the Mss. which I had, let them to make these reflections; the fear of losing them prevailed over the scruple, and Darab consented to what I desired.

Their fears were not ill-founded. Mancherji himself, knowing the use which I had made of his manuscript, was no more tranquil than Darab. He feared lest Dustoor Bikh (Bhicáji?) his teacher should have been informed of it. Seeing that I kept it many months, he demanded it from

* A rich and influential Mobed and an agent at the Dutch Factory.—*Translator.*

me through the head of the Dutch Factory to whom he had lent it. My answer was polite and steady. I stated to M. Taillefer that having commenced to note down the differences, which existed in the manuscript of Mancherji and that of my Dustoors, it was not natural that I would leave the work imperfect. My reasons did not please the Dutch, with whom I had not been much in contact for the last month or two. They came almost to menaces. I even knew that a member of their council, a mischievous head, was instigated to come to my house with a band of soldiers to carry away the book in question. The Chief of the Dutch Factory (M. Taillefer), being more prudent, did not wish to descend to practical matters. He was a man of letters, and I am sure that at the bottom, he blamed not my firmness, though he was obliged to show to his broker, that he was prepared to render such service as was required of him. The only precaution which I took was to have upon my table two charged pistols ; I continued my work which lasted four months, after which I returned the Ms. in good state.

The scruple of the Parsi Dustoors being surmounted, and their little tricks having ended, there remained with me nothing to overcome but the peculiar difficulties attendant on the kind of study which I had commenced, and the unavoidable embarrassment of a civil war. The English then laid siege to the fortress: it was necessary to put in security their own effects and those of the factory—being always in a state of diffidence and distrust. These troubles made my Dustoors more distant from me. They reappeared after some time.

Finding myself sufficiently strong to commence the study of the Zend books, and impatient to regain the months, which I had seen glide away in the midst of these troubles, without making any tangible progress, I spent some days in the practice of reading the Vendidad, and to translate from the Persian interlineary translation the Pehlvi and Persian vocabulary of which I have spoken above.

The work, the first of the kind which a European had ever attempted, appeared to me to be a notable event in the history of literature; and I marked its date which was the 24th March 1759 of the era of Jesus Christ, Amerdád, the seventh day of the month of Meher, 1128 of the era of Yezdegird, 1172 of the Hijra, and 1813 of the reign of Rájá Vikramajit. The commencement was sufficiently discouraging; but I had learned at much cost to keep patience. Hoping to succeed in the work which I had undertaken, I informed the Governor of Pondichery of the success of my attempts.

After having obtained some Zend and Sanscrit books, I commenced the translation of the Vendidad, on the 30th of March 1759. Modern Persian served me as an intermediate language, because Darab, for fear of being heard by my domestics, did not wish to unfold to me the mysteries of his religion in the vulgar language. I wrote everything; I was also particular in marking the reading of Zend and of Pehlvi in European characters. I compared afterwards the pieces, which appeared to be the same, in order to assure myself of the correctness of his (Darab's) readings. The most grievous accidents and sickness, howsoever long it might be, had nothing to frighten me. I was always in a state to take up again my studies at the point where I had last left them; and being assured against the fear of forgetting them, the tranquillity of my mind could only hasten my recovery.

These precautions were only too necessary; and they

had the desired effect. My health was many times the victim of close application to my study and to the kind of life I led. A dish of rice and lentils was all my nourishment. The time, which was not engaged with my Dustoor, I spent in revising what I had read with him, and preparing the work for the next day. I could not take even a nap after dinner, as is generally done in warm countries: for, one time it had served as an excuse for the absence of Darab, who pretended that I did not open the door when he knocked it. In the evening I refreshed myself an hour or two with an airing on my terrace, the mind always occupied with the uncertainty of the success of my researches, and the manner in which they would be received in Europe.

In the midst of this stiff work, I did not neglect to augment my knowledge of those countries in which I could not then penetrate, viz., the north of India and Egypt: but a sad accident checked me at the commencement of my career.

While assisting one day the lifting up of a trunk which contained all my luggage, I saw one of the coolies employed in the work miss his footing and on the point of being crushed. I seized immediately one of its handles, and held it suspended for a moment whilst the coolie rose up. I did not then feel any derangement in my system, but after some time, close study, coupled with great heat (it being the month of June), made the malady burst out—the cause being the exertion I had made: it was what they called at Surat *the derangement of the navel.*

This complaint consists in the looseness of the umbilical vessels, whose extremities form the knot which is in the middle of the belly. If this looseness make the arteries rise above the knot, one is subjected to continual vomitings; and when the derangement is below or towards the side, it is followed by frequent purging which, in a few days, brings the patient to the last extremity. * * *

It appeared that I could foresee the state in which I would soon be, if I endeavoured to prosecute my work, the most insipid imaginable. In the morning I collated Mancherji's Ms. with Darab's copy ; and during the afternoon, when the heat was greatest, I translated the Vendidad from the last Ms. These two works were finished on the 16th June 1759. I announced this event to M. de Leyrit in my letter of the 11th June, while requesting him to procure for me a copy of the four Vedas (the sacred books of the Hindoos) through the medium of Aranga Poulley or Arombale. But no sooner had I commenced translating the additional passages I had found in Mancherji's Ms. than I was again attacked with a more severe bowel complaint. After two days of acute griping, it became necessary to send for the Parsi,* who had already given me an experience of the force of his muscles...........I passed the end of July in a state of forced inaction, which grieved me more than the fear of having to recall the aid of the Parsi. Some letters to M. de Leyrit and the revision of my works were all I did. As I had only to write the translation and read Zend and Pehlvi books, my mind was sufficiently at ease. * * * *

While I was among the English, I engaged Nanabhâi, their Modi, to procure from Nowsaree a copy of the *Nirengastân* brought to India by Dustoor Jamasp. On the

* A quack adept at curing this particular complaint. Men of the sort are even now to be found practising in Surat and also in Bombay, but they are not necessarily Parsis.—*Translator*.

7th October, this Parsi showed me the answer which he had received, stating that it was not known what had become of that work.

Finding my strength recovered, I made search for a house where I might resume my occupation freely; and they found me one in which I went to live, still remaining under the English protection. My wounds* were entirely healed on the 20th November; and I applied myself at once to the translation of the Zend books with Darab. I commenced with the additional passages discovered in Mancherji's Ms. The translation of these passages was followed by that of Yaçna, of Vispered, of Nyâesh and Yashts and some Pehlvi collections, which contained, among other curious pieces, the Bundehesh, the Si-rozáh, the Vajerkerd, several Ravâets and other Persian Mss. which Darab had given me. A sustained application to these gave me, at the end of some months, so true a notion of the languages and of the ancient history, religion and usages of the Parsis, that Darab dared not and even could not impose upon me; and by the time that he had ceased his readings, I was in a state to translate myself the few works which yet remained to be translated. He was now regular, and ventured not to refuse me the explanations I demanded from him.

The departure of Mr. Spencer, and the state in which I knew our factories were, contributed much to the rapidity of my progress. I did not stir out, because I feared that the taking of Pondichery would arrest the progress of my studies; I pushed on my work in some way.

---

* The author refers here to the wounds he had received in a duel with a Frenchman, which arose from a petty cause.—*Translator.*

I had derived some advantage from my sojourn among the English by attracting to myself a part of the credit which they had in the city (Surat). Fares Khan lent me, at the recommendation of Mr. Spencer, his copy of the Barzo-Námeh, the only one which was at Surat; and I made a copy from it. Mr. Spencer, before leaving Surat, was kind enough to undertake to send from Delhi to the Vakeel of the English East India Company the list of books which I required. These were the four Vedas in Sanscrit, the latter part of the Barzo-Námeh, a series of well-preserved coins of Rupees, struck by the order of Nour Jehán Begum, wife of Jehanghir, bearing each a mark of one of the signs of the Zodiac, some historical books on India and (Independent) Tartary, and especially the Persian translation of the four Vedas, made by Feize, brother of Abulfazel, secretary to Akbar. I had also requested, in November, Mr. Erskine, a member of the council of Surat, who spoke the Moorish (Mahomedan) language very well, and who went to command at Tattah in Sinde, to buy on my account some natural curiosities which that country could offer him. He was also requested to copy out for me the inscriptions which were said to be engraved on the walls of a famous temple near Tattah, built, according to the opinion of its inhabitants, by Alexander; to search for me some charts of the mountains of Candáhár; and to send me some Sanscrit, Sindee, and Patani books if they fell in his hands. I had no news of my commission till September 1760, when Mr. Erskine wrote to me from Sinde that there were neither temples, nor ancient monuments, nor Hindoo inscriptions about the environs of Tattah; but that there were some tombs of the kings of Sinde with some Arabic or Persian inscriptions almost effaced. He promised to send me afterwards some books and charts. Though this short answer of his could not satisfy me much, I availed myself of the offer made at the end of his letter, and wrote to him for the books I wanted. These were (independent of those which Mr. Spencer had written to me about from Delhi) *Madar ul Afazel*—a Persian Dictionary highly esteemed, the complete *Rozot-ossafâ*, some memoirs of the Rájás Jessing and Jessonsing, on Cashmere and Candáhár, the *Nadershâh Námeh* (history of Tamas Kouli Khan), a list of Indian kings from Gengiskhan, with their details, and also that of the Rájás of Delhi whom they have succeeded; the Tatar alphabet, the *Serûd Námeh*, a treatise on vocal and instrumental music, composed by Abou Aloufah; the *Tasvir Námeh*, a Persian translation of a work on perspective and painting made by Ebn Hossein.

All these requests excited the surprise and procured for me the friendship of the persons to whom I had applied for the aforesaid books. They procured me many promises, but not one of them produced the desired effect. Mr. Erskine wrote to me, on the 8th November of the same year, from Máhim, near Bombay, where he had gone to recruit his health, that he had thought on his return from Sinde, to procure me the books I wanted; and that though he believed that the inscriptions, of which he had spoken to me, were only passages of the Korân, he would try to take copies of those, which were inscribed on two or three tombs of the ancient kings of Sinde and send them on to me. The death of this gallant gentleman deprived me of the fruit of his promises.

* * * *

At last I received, in the middle of April, a letter from the Governor of Pondichery, dated 24th February 1760, which permitted me to return to the French Residency. I thanked the English councils of Surat and Bombay for the protection which they had so obligingly accorded me, and placed myself again under the protection of the banner of my nation, without quitting the mansion which I had inhabited, and which was more commodious than the French Residency.

I rapidly advanced in the knowledge of the mysteries of the language, and of the history of the Parsis. I found from day to day that I ought to buy some new book or other. Backed with the authority of M. de Leyrit, my brother supported with all his influence the propositions which I made to my Dustoors. Besides, as they were aware that I was soon to depart from them, they dared no longer refuse me anything. They employed a thousand means to render themselves useful to me, to protract my departure and to increase the price of the manuscripts.

* * * * *

The reading of the liturgical books had made me familiar with some minor ceremonies of the Zoroastrian religion; I had bought some copper instruments used in their sacred rites by the Parsis, some Koshtis, a Sudrá and a Padân. but my curiosity was not satisfied. I wished to enter their Fire-temple and to attend their service. Being aware of the strict severity of their religion, I believed the thing impossible: my presence, according to the Zend books, would defile the temple and tend to nullify the efficacy of their prayers. Besides, no foreigner had ever entered the Derémehers* of the Parsis, except the Mogul Emperor, Akbar. However, a small present and the promise to take a short

* For the explanation of this term, see Mr. K. R. Cama's "Discourse on the Mithraic worship and the rites and mysteries connected with it", pp. 22—23.—*Translator.*

excursion through the town in my palanquin, induced Darab to satisfy my curiosity. He took for this purpose a rainy day, the 20th June, 1760. I was dressed as a Parsi, accompanied by only one peon, who was made to stand at a short distance from the gate of the Derémeher, and who guided me from a sufficient distance for fear I should be recognised—the environs of the Fire-temple being inhabited by a number of Parsis. The water was knee-deep in several places; it was all dark, and as I was not sufficiently acquainted with all the streets of Surat, I was on the point of losing my way and of being nearly drowned.

When I arrived at the Derémeher, there were very few people in it. Darab came to receive me, and led me to the fire-altar where his son officiated: it was half past six in the evening, in the *Aiviçruthrem Geh.*

Old Darab, notwithstanding the objections which I had sometimes raised against what I had found to be unreasonable in his religion, had seen me study his books with so much care, and occupy myself so seriously with the smallest minutæ, instead of despising them, as is generally the case with foreigners, that he believed me almost a proselyte, wanting only the ceremonies of initiation; and I think that this idea consoled his conscience a little. Several times he had persuaded me to give up smoking my Hookkâ, saying, that I had read in the Parsi books that what came out from the body, as saliva, breath, defiled the fire. Instead of contradicting him boldly—which would have displeased him—I contented myself with the reply that *I was a Christian.* When I was in presence of the sacred fire, which I saw like all lay Parsis across the rails, which enclosed the chapel on the north side, Darab asked me if I would make some offering to it. I said I could not, as a Christian, comply with his request. Darab retorted, but with an embarrassed air which had something sinister about it, that some Musulmans, without having had the privilege of seeing the sacred fire, had made some presents to the Derémèher. The position was delicate: I was alone, without any arms except my sabre and a pocket-pistol; and if the devotees, who performed their prayers in the Derémèher, had suspected me who I was, I should have fallen a victim to the zeal of the worshippers of the Fire-temple. Without appearing in any way moved, I answered Darab in a loud voice, that I was come to see the Derémèher and nothing more. My firmness shut up his mouth; he requested me to speak in a lower tone; he feared more than myself that the people of the Derémèher might recognise me. He explained to me afterwards, in a whisper, the use made of the different parts of the Derémèher. I examined everything minutely. I entered everywhere; and I imprinted very clearly in my mind all that I saw, in order to be able to prepare on my return the plan and the description which will be seen hereafter in the second volume, pp. 568—572.

After having attentively inspected the divisions of the Derémèher, I approached, with a view to satisfy my curiosity, the place reserved for the recital of Izeshné (Yaçna). Darab made some difficulty to allow me to enter it, protesting that he would afterwards be obliged to purify the place; but I went further on and found in a corner of the *Izeshné-gáh* his Zend, Pehlvi and Persian books, and among others, some Mss. which he had told me he had not with him. I knew that his library was in the Derémèher, and this was one of the reasons which had induced me to enter this temple with the view to an inquiry in reference thereto.

Satisfied with my visit which lasted nearly an hour, I rejoined my peon, who was waiting for me within gun-shot from the Derémeher. Darab, deceived in his expectations, had no occasion to be equally satisfied. He had calculated on extracting from me something as an offering to the sacred fire; and the discovery which I had made put him to the necessity, if he did not wish to fall out with me, to sell the books which he had up to then denied me, or refused to make copies of for me.

Some time after I went out of Surat to see the *Dakhmas* (towers of silence). These are a species of round towers whose walls are built of square stones, and which are about ninety feet in diameter. While I walked round these towers, whose walls were assailed by an army of vultures, ravens and other carnivorous birds, several Parsis, who saw me from a distance, grumbled at my curiosity. In the mean time a funeral procession arrived, which obliged me to remain at a distance. From the place where I stood, I saw the *Nasâsâlârs* perform the *Sagdid** (that is to say, the ceremony of presenting the dog to the dead), and carry the dead body into the *Dakhma*. Afterwards the procession, which stood at more than eighty paces from the spot, returned, praying two by two, each holding the other by his sleeve,† as they had done while going. On my return their murmurs increased: in the streets of Surat many Parsis loudly clamoured that I had profaned their towers of silence; but these complaints had no other consequences,

---

* It is not the Nasâsâlârs who perform the ceremony above referred to, but the Zoroastrian, who is the resident guardian of the Dakhma.—*Translator.*

† Now-a-days it is usual to hold a handkerchief between two persons.—*Translator.*

and whilst I felt myself in good spirits, I went to see the place where the Hindoos burnt their dead.

*　　　*　　　*　　　*　　　*

I finished, in September 1760, what concerned the Parsis and the translation of their sacred books, and then went to the French Residency, in order to prepare myself for a journey which I had contemplated long since, and which had connection with Parsis and Hindoos alike.

*　　　*　　　*　　　*　　　*

I started from Surat on the 18th November 1760, at 2 o'clock in the afternoon, accompanied with four sepoys and one servant (who, with the coolies formed a cortege of thirteen men) and furnished with paper, a pair of compasses, some pistols and two pass-ports, one from the Nabob, and the other from the Maráthás.

With this retinue I passed through Lájpore, Nowsáree, Gandévi, Bulsár, Oodwárá, Colek, Daman, Nárgor, Sanján, Tárápore and Bassein. This journey occupied about ten days. Thence I came down to Kenéry to make a minute survey of its caves and copy out its inscriptions. This work, which kept me engaged till the 6th December, being finished I came to Táná, where I felt myself indisposed. Fever came over me on the 9th December with cold fits and lasted three days, which I passed on my bed drinking nothing but tea. When I was in a state to sit on the chair, I occupied myself in fairly copying out the Kenéry inscriptions and a part of the diary of my journey written briefly, while the different objects were yet fresh in my memory. After having finished this business, I waited for two days to see if my health would recover; but a fresh attack of fever and the shortness of my funds obliged me to quit Táná.

I set out on the 16th December 1760, and followed the same route which I had taken while coming from Surat. Only beyond Bassein I took my way a little to the east, and went below the Ghauts in search of the seeds of the teak and champa trees. This last effort exhausted me; I was seized with a burning fever, which forced me to take some hours of repose at Agâsi.

The fever took me back beyond Agâsi; and, whilst fully perspiring, I had the folly to cause some cold water to be thrown on my head, and my men had the simplicity to obey me. This imprudence had no effect: the fever continued, and I arrived at Bulsár, without having eaten anything since my departure from Agâsi. There, seeing my palanquin-bearers eat some large horse-raddishes, I felt a desire to taste them. They brought me one of an inch and a half in diameter, which I ate with salt with sufficient appetite and without being incommoded in any way. At Gandévi the fever quitted me after a light repast of lentils and rice, and I then slept for two or three hours, which I had not done since eight days.

When I arrived at Nowsáree, I begged Dustoor Jamsheed to come and see me in the garden where I wanted to pass the night. My reputation had already spread all over that town. The Dustoor came to me at ten o'clock in the night. We talked in Persian and Pehlvi; he avowed to me that Darab, whose conduct he otherwise blamed, was the most clever Dustoor in India, and also assured me that he had not the *Nirengustán* which was brought from Kirman by Dustoor Jamasp. The conversation ended in reciprocal marks of amity, and he promised to write to me at Surat, which he did, after some months, in Persian and Pehlvi.

I arrived at Surat after eight days' march, enfeebled and almost without consciousness. My return gave my brother evident pleasure: the length of my journey had disquieted him. As for me, in a moment of calmness, the dangers I had run and the fatigues I had endured, presenting themselves vividly and *en masse* to my mind, drew tears from my eyes; my friends wiped them off, and four days of repose and good nourishment made all the symptoms of fever disappear.

But this appearance of health made only some moments bright for me. In the first days of January 1761, frightful colics, accompanied with pains in the fingers and the right cheek, which was believed to be caused by the gout, obliged me, after vain efforts, to confine myself to bed. Patience was my physician; the diet, and, without doubt, the remaining strength of my youth overcame the disease; but I was in a state of weakness, which determined me to renounce my journey to Benares and China. Besides, the state of our affairs would have frustrated all my plans, even if my strength had yielded to my desire. Pondichery being besieged, succour of every kind missed us; for several years the Residency of Surat had not received any funds from the chief Factory (at Pondichery); my brother had difficulty in supporting himself, and could not absolutely take upon himself any expense on my account. What means to adopt in this extremity?

I possessed more than 180 Mss. in nearly all the languages of India; among others two copies of the works of Zoroaster and a part of Pehlvi books; seven dictionaries of modern Persian, and three most famous Sanscrit dictionaries of India. I had some Hindoo characters of an extremely remote time in the Kenéry inscriptions, some Sanscrit letters, very ancient, in the first pages of the extracts of the Vedas, some others 300 years old in the translations of some works of Zoroaster, and also some Tamoul letters a thousand years old in the characters used by the Jews of Cochin. I shall not talk of the seeds, flowers and leaves of trees which I had collected for myself at great expense; several other natural curiosities, some instruments connected with the ceremonies of the Parsi religion, and a collection, sufficiently considerable, of the coins of India.

The peril to which all these literary treasures as well as my own labours were about to be exposed, and the languishing state in which I was, determined me to return to France, deferring to some more favourable opportunity the translation of the Vedas, the explication of Indian Antiquities and the series of researches, which I had intended to make on the different religions of these countries.

* * * * *

But it was decreed that my departure from India should be of the same stamp as that from Paris: that it must be beset with as many difficulties as the rest of my works, which had detained me nearly for six years in this country.

All my affairs being arranged, as far as the critical position in which we were at Surat could permit, I prepared myself to quit this city, and already my luggage and effects were on board ship, which was to carry me to Bombay, when I learned that a question had been raised to disembark them, and that I had been accused before the English Consul with carrying away Mss. for which I had not paid. The affair went to deprive me of the fruit of a hard work, at a time when I was on the point of enjoying it. This stroke astonished, but did not disconcert me. I guessed the hand which had wrought it. Dustoor Kaous had never approved of the complaisance of his son Darab, who, in despair of seeing me part so soon, flattered himself to be able, by means of the English on whom he then relied, to arrest my effects or at least to oblige me to pay him a considerable sum of money, as damages for the period for which he had made an engagement with me. The taking of Pondichery emboldened them: the French name appeared annihilated in India. It then became necessary to prove that all that I was about to carry to Europe belonged legitimately to me. The altercation took place in the presence of the English Consul; it was sharp; I threatened the Consul with carrying the affair to Bombay, and summoning him there in person. I was in such moments of despair, when one does not respect anything. The English easily discovered that the Parsi Dustoors sought only to check the transport of their books to Europe or at least to take advantage of the predicament in which they found us. To cut their prosecution short, my brother stood bail for me; and when they saw that the English were satisfied with his word, they disappeared. These annoyances brought on a complaint of gout, and I passed in bed the little time which elapsed before the departure of the ship.

It was on the 15th March 1761, that I left Surat in an enfeebled state which the sea-voyage only increased, with no other resource but the kindness of our enemies, and the credit bill which my brother had passed me; and moved to find that it was impossible for me to recognise the services of my domestics, of the people of the French

Residency and of the interpreter Maneckji, and even to remunerate, as I believed they merited, Dustoors Darab and Kaous, whose ill proceedings I had already forgotten.

The voyage was short and tranquil; I was with a gallant man, Captain Purling; I always tried not to be troublesome. We anchored in Bombay harbour on the 16th of March, and I soon came ashore with the captain.

I shall not stop here to give a description of Bombay; this island is sufficiently known by the accounts given of it by English travellers. It has a length of about two hours' walk from the end of the harbour of Mahim, which is connected on the side of Salsette with Bandora; and one and a half hours' walk in breadth. The length is from north to south-west. On the side of the open sea Bombay was formerly covered with cocoa-trees and bamboo-trees, which formed a part of its revenue and gave the most beautiful umbrage: but at the same time the rotten fish and shell-fish, which the people made use of to manure the ground and the trunks of these trees, rendered the air of this island very unhealthy. Before the last war, the fear of the French obliged them to cut these trees to clear the environs of the town which is otherwise very badly fortified.

The castle is not of any use for defence. The only strength of Bombay against the invasion of Europeans is in its harbour. It is there also that the English show themselves off. Every thing there is in an admirable order. The house of the commissioner of the navy is the first which one sees on that side: it is beautiful and commodious, and communicates with the harbour by a back-door. The magazines and the arsenal are a little distant and above the sea.

On the other side is the gate of the custom-house, presided over by a councillor who has his mansion in the compound there. The wealth of the people and the bulk of merchandise which lie in the yards and the store-houses, characterise well a people whose element is commerce.

These are the two places which form Bombay Proper, together with all the other English establishments. The Governor, who has only to sanction the acts which emanate from him and to preside from time to time at the council, has a palace in the black town where he seldom resides. He lives more at Parell in a magnificent country-house, converted from an old church in the shape of a cross, having terraces and gardens. Several councillors have also their country-houses out of town, in sandy and open places. The one then best situated was that of Mr. Bysill, the second man in Bombay. It is built on a rock, commanding the sea, on the side of the mark of the steerage, on which the vessels direct their course whilst entering the harbour. In the afternoon this mansion was the rendezvous of the principal men of the colony who went there for tea.

Bombay, lying between Mocha, Basráh, Surat and the Malabar side, would be nothing but for its situation and its harbour. But were the English to find means to make the Maráthás cede Salsette to them, the island of Bombay, independent of its revenue, would become one of the finest establishments in India, on account of all the pleasures of life which one finds in Salsette, and which would compensate for the dryness and sterility of this important island.

I had no other lodging at Bombay than the house of Mr. Spencer, the then commissioner of the navy; this added to the services which he had rendered me at Surat. He conferred this new favour by contriving to render my stay supportable in a town which I saw filled up with French prisoners. The arrival of the squadron, commanded by Admiral Stevens, was the occasion of feastings in the mansions of the Governor Crommelin and Mr. Spencer. I was several times at those feasts where they treated me with every regard which politeness and humanity could prescribe towards an enemy whom they wished to oblige.

During the last days which I passed at Bombay, I had several conversations with Mr. Spencer on the settlements of Europeans in India. If ever a man was qualified to reconcile parties animated against each other, it was this generous Englishman. I told him that if the Companies entrusted their interests to these two gentlemen of recognised probity, viz., to himself and M. de Leyrit, one would see perhaps the quarrels subside. Mr. Spencer sincerely wished to see amity between the two nations; but he always recurred to the large possessions of the French and their conquests; this made me think that he disapproved of these operations. Notwithstanding the moderation and strict honesty which guarded his conversation, I believed he was of opinion that the pre-eminence and even the extension of commerce, in a nation different from his own, was a sort of crime.

Mr. Spencer had kindly wished to give me a large map of the interior and of the south coasts of the peninsula, made by the Brahmins; I succeeded in making a copy of it, and being ready to leave India, I felt inclined to open my heart to him, as to the doubt which I had regarding the genuineness of the Mss. I was carrying to Europe. I told him then, that having lost in Bengal the copy of the first lines of the Zend Ms. of Oxford which I had brought from Europe, I knew not if my Mss. contained similar lines to them. Mr. Spencer tranquillized me fully on this subject, by pointing out a means which he asked me to keep secret. He himself afterwards made some arrangement about my passage, with the Captain of the *Bristol* which was ready to set sail to Europe, and paid him for that one thousand rupees, and gave me twelve hundred rupees in cash and in bills on Mr. Hough, his correspondent in London. These sums were in advance of the amount of the letter of which I have talked above.* I endorsed this letter, remitted it to him, and he undertook to get it cashed after my departure. I gave my word that there was nothing in my papers which treated on what they call state affairs, relative to the quarrels which then divided the two nations; and he put the seal of the Company on my effects, which were delivered over in that state to the Captain of the *Bristol.*

I left Bombay on the 28th April 1761, heaped with the obliging attentions of Mr. Spencer, of the Governor Crommelin, of every Englishman, and especially of those whom I had known at Surat. The vessel set sail on the same day that I went on board of it; it carried to England many French officers as captives, whom the squadron had brought from the Coromandel Coast.

Let one portray to himself cold and deliberate cruelty, coupled with baseness of soul with a sordid interest, and he will have the picture of Captain Quicke with whom I voyaged to Europe. The voyage was analogous to his character. He went to the length of giving us salted meat and crumbs of biscuits, which formed all our nourishment.

---

* This refers to a promissory note, which his brother had received from one of his countrymen in consideration of a sum of money, which the former had advanced to the latter.—*Translator*.

* * * * *

We anchored at the port of Portsmouth on the 17th November 1761. Before the vessel entered it, several sailors of the Royal Navy, who had returned from India, fled in a small boat to escape the Laws of the *Press,* according to which they would be forced, after having passed ten years out of their country, to go back immediately in other vessels and to recommence the service, without having the liberty to embrace their wives and children.

* * * *

On the 20th November, I started for Wickham, a large borough 12 miles from Portsmouth, where several of my friends, Irish officers in the service of France, had kept a bed for me. Here, after some days, finding myself short of money, I sent to Mr. Hough at London the bill of Mr. Spencer, and passed the days in my little habitation, occupied in preparing a list of the Mss. which I had intended for *la Bibliotheque du Roi,* and in putting in order a brief account of my literary works. Some solitary promenades and one or two visits to two Englishmen of rank, whose splendid country-mansions were near Wickham, were all my relaxation from work. Inquietude, together with my retired habits and perhaps the change of climate, brought on me tertian fever, from which two bleedings freed me.

During this time I received a letter from Mr. Thomas Birch, Secretary to the Royal Society, dated London 7th January, 1762. I had written to him on the 27th November and 23rd December, praying him to take an interest as a man of letters in my situation, and especially to send me the copy of the first leaves of the Ms. of Zoroaster which was at Oxford, if it was not permitted to me to go there personally to consult this work. After some excuses for the delay in answer, caused by my first letter not having reached him, Mr. Birch wrote to me, that the Royal Society had no power over the University of Oxford, which would not allow any of its Mss. to be carried to such a distance (viz., to London or Wickham). He added that if I would write to him more in detail the circumstances of my detention, he would do all in his power to obtain me the permission to go to Oxford.

This very obliging offer came too late, but it gave me a favourable idea of the *savants* to whom I was ready to pay a visit.

My journey being determined upon, I took from Mr. Garnier* letters of recommendation to Dr. Swinton, Principal of the Winchester College and to Dr. Barton, Canon of Christ College at Oxford. I had received, on the 13th January, from Mr. Eddowes, to whom I had given information of the change of my place, his most flattering compliments. He assured me at the same time that he would transmit me on his part a letter to Dr. Warton, Professor of Poesy; and that generally I would be recommended to all the *savants* of the University. Furnished with these pass-ports, more necessary in one way for the success of my journey than the pass-port of the Board for sick sailors &c., I parted from Wickham, on the 14th January, carrying with me some Hindoo works and three best Zend Mss. intended for *la Bibliotheque du Roi,* namely, the Vendidad Sádé, the Zend and Pehlvi Vendidad and the volume which contained the Zend and Sanscrit Yaçna and Yashts Sádé. I thought it would be fair to show a part of my riches to

---

* A friend who had assisted Mon. Anquetil in many ways.—*Translator*.

persons whose aid I was about to solicit for opening their treasures to me.

Arrived at Oxford, my first care was to know where Dr. Swinton lived. I was shown his residence, and I delivered to him the letter, which procured me a very gracious reception, and which also announced the object of my journey. Having offered a cup of tea, he conducted me to Dr. Barton, who we found was not at his place.

Thence we went to the Bodleian Library, where they showed me the Vendidad Sádé, attached to a chain, in a particular place. The weather was very cold; and I wished to carry the Ms. to my inn in order to compare it with my copy. The proposition was not accepted; Dr. Browne, Vice-Chancellor of the University and custodian of the Library, told me that I would be allowed to examine it at ease in the Library only. I promised to go there the next day, and cast a glance at the building which was oblong, a little high and sufficiently sombre, and the interior of which formed an inverted H.

The next day, the 18th January, I went to the Bodleian Library, at 9 o'clock, where, notwithstanding the cold which was very biting, I passed an hour in examining the Vendidad Sádé, taking a copy of the notice of it, written in the Zend characters, which one can see in the list of the Zend Mss. deposited at *la Bibliotheque du Roi.* I gave this information to the librarian, who had another copy of it less exact, in which the name of the *Júd dév dád* (which is the same as the Vendidad) was substituted for that of the author.

After having assured myself that the best of my Mss. was the same as the Zend Ms. of the Bodleian Library, I expressed to Dr. Swinton my desire to see the Mss. of Dr. Hyde and those of Mr. Fraser. These were in the hands of Dr. Hunt, Professor of Arabic, who was then charged with putting them in order for the Radcliffe Library. I went, then, conducted by Dr. Swinton to this Doctor, who offered politely to show them to me at 3 o'clock. I accepted the offer and went to Dr. Barton, who waited for me at dinner, with my *cicéroné*, Dr. Swinton. The repast was homely; but I observed with sorrow the humble manner in which Dr. Swinton sat in the presence of Dr. Bartcn, who was in the enjoyment of an income in benefices more than 30,000 francs. We drank to the good success of the works of Zoroaster, and I strongly induced these gentlemen to renew the connection, which the *savants* of England formerly had with those of France. These words pleased them: they told me that I was the first Frenchman, whom they remembered to have seen at Oxford for an object purely relating to the progress of human knowledge; they exhorted me at the same time to make known their sentiments to my compatriots; and Mrs. and Miss Barton supported what the doctors said. After taking coffee, Dr. Barton, who was a member of the Society of Antiquaries, wished to give me a specimen of his work. He then carried us to his study and showed to Dr. Swinton, the Apollo of rich doctors, a drawer full of medals, on which he asked his opinion. This occasioned some *impromptus* on antiquity, after which we went to Dr. Hunt, whom we found muffled up in his robe. As there was no time at hand, after the first compliments, he went to search the Mss. of Dr. Hyde, referred to in the list already cited, and told me that he knew the ancient Persian language. But without insisting upon the fact I made him understand that the Mss. (viz., the Viráf Námeh and the Sadder), which he read by means of a Zend and Persian alphabet, found by him in the Ms. of the Nyâesh belonging to Dr. Hyde, and which he had shown to me and taken for the ancient Persian, were nothing more than modern Persian clothed in the characters of the old Persian (Zend) language. The science of Dr. Hunt was at a loss before the book of the Nyâesh of this Doctor; and in order to convince him, I opened the three folio-books which I had brought with me. He admired the character in which they were written and the state in which they were preserved, but could absolutely read nothing. I showed him in one of these three books the Nyâesh, a copy of which he had before him, and added that Mr. Fraser had brought with him other works of a similar character of which I mentioned to him the names. It was Dustoor Shapoor who had informed me of these particulars, when I was at Surat, and who had assured me that this Englishman (Mr. Fraser) knew neither Zend nor Pehlvi, but that he spoke a little Persian. Surprised to see me so well instructed, Dr. Hunt went to search the Mss. of Mr. Fraser, which were in the character which I had spoken to him about, and from which I copied the notices in Persian.

Much satisfied with the complaisance and civilities of Dr. Hunt, I left him for my inn; but Dr. Swinton induced me to pass a minute at his house. There I found a bachelor who had applied himself to the history of Bactria. Mrs. Swinton, a young Genevese lady, talking French very well, gave me a most gracious reception, and her husband presented me a medal of one of the Kings of Persia, of a type similar to the several copies represented at its commencement in the work of Dr. Hyde on the religion of the Parsis: on one side of it is to be seen the head of a king, and on the other a censer of fire put on a pedestal resembling an altar. Willing or unwilling it was necessary that I should tell him what I could read thereon. In vain did I declare that the characters engraved on it were partly effaced and partly different from Zend letters: it was all taken for a shift. Then, sorry at not being able to recognise otherwise the trouble which Dr. Swinton had taken for me, I tried to decipher the legend and acquaint him with what I for the moment believed to be its true signification. This good Doctor conducted me back to my inn. He had had the complaisance to accompany me everywhere the two days that I passed at Oxford. I felt in embracing him a real sorrow that he was not more opulent.

I arrived in London on the 31st January. After having made necessary arrangements for my passage to France, I occupied myself in London, till the day of my departure, with seeing such sights as could excite the curiosity of a stranger.

While returning from the Museum, I went up to Dr. Morton. This Doctor has acquired a reputation by the publication of Tables of Hebrew, Greek and Arabic alphabets of different ages. He made me present of a copy of those published, and showed me a draft of different Sanscrit alphabets, very defective, which he was getting engraved. He pretended having in his possession the Zend alphabet, because he had in his collection some characters which resembled Zend letters; I removed this misimpression from his mind, for which he appeared to be pleased with me, by informing him that the value he put on these characters was absolutely different from that of the real in the Zend alphabet. In fact, if it were enough that the two characters should resemble, because one came from the other, or be identical, one would trace the Roman, Hebrew and Indian letters even to Mexican Hieroglyphics. I left Dr. Morton much satisfied with his politeness as well as with that of other *savants* of the Museum, with whom I could have wished that my affairs had permitted me to converse for a longer time, as well as with the Doctors of Oxford.

* * * *

I arrived at Paris on the 14th March 1762, and soon forgot in the embrace of a father nearly seventy years old, and of brothers whom I loved tenderly, the fatigues of a journey as long as it was perilous. On the next day, the 15th March, I deposited with *la Bibliotheque du Roi* the works of Zoroaster and other Mss. which I had destined for this precious treasury. Gratitude conducted me afterwards to the persons who had interested themselves in my journey and had patronised it. I found in M. l'Abbé Barthelemy an obliging *savant* and, what touched me most, a friend. M. le Comte de Caylus, M. Lamoignon de Malesherbes and M. Bignon received me with a sort of tenderness. The minister (M. le Comte de Saint-Florentin) willingly paid me the homage due to my works and showered on me the graces of the King. The *savants* whom I had seen at Paris before my departure, and those, to whom M. l'Abbé Barthelemy introduced me, were eager to testify to me the joy which my return had caused them. Soon the noise of my travels, and the importance of the Mss. which I had deposited with *la Bibliotheque du Roi,* fixed on me the attention of persons of the first rank. M. le Duc de Choiseul, M. le Comte de la Guiche and M. de Saint Simon, bishop of Agde, gave me the most favourable reception. Encouraged by these flattering marks of a general approbation, and yielding to the earnestness of the public, and even of strangers whose curiosity had been excited by the announcement of the works which I had brought, I thought since then to put in order the translations and the literary researches, which had occupied me in the course of my travels.

I had passed nearly eight years out of my native country and nearly six in India. I returned in 1762, poorer than when I parted from Paris in 1754, my inheritance having gone in my travels to add to the smallness of my salary. But I was rich in rare and ancient records and learning, which my youth (I was hardly thirty years old) gave me time to edit at leisure; and this was all the fortune in search of which I had gone to India.

India is a fertile country which will always offer to the real *savant,* as well as to the ordinary spectator, abundant harvest of objects of researches, equally useful and interesting. I have gleaned information in an age in which the resources did not always correspond to my courage, and at a time in which the fury of war had devastated the best provinces. Let us admit in good faith, (that is a result which my feeble efforts can lead to)—let us admit that whilst we move continually some leagues of ground thousand times searched, the largest part of the globe is yet left unknown to us. Ye learned and daring travellers! let us take no more the reach of our view for the measure of the universe; let us venture to cross the Ghauts, the Cordilleras, in order to know where we are on our way: the summits of these lofty mountains will show us an immense space which yet remains to us to run over.

EXTRACTS

FROM THE

LIFE OF ZOROASTER.

Before reading the works of a Personage so celebrated as. Zoroaster, we can only view with pleasure the details regarding his life and legislation; and even considered in this respect, the circumstances, which otherwise appear most immaterial, present to the reader a degree of importance which renders them interesting; they excite a sort of curiosity which it is just to satisfy.

The Greeks, Latins and Orientals concur in representing Zoroaster as a genius of the first order, an extraordinary man; but all of them do not enter into details regarding him. My object is to relate here what the books of the Parsis have informed me of their Legislator, but without guaranteeing the testimony, always suspicious, of the people whose interest it is to extol him whose laws they follow: and in order not to omit anything that might serve to make him better known, I shall take care to compare the traits, which the Greeks and Latins furnish us. The reflections which I shall indulge in will ordinarily depend on these different authorities. Such is the course which criticism would prescribe to itself on a subject, in which for many considerations, there are just as good reasons for rejecting as for accepting any testimony.

* * * * * †

† Here the learned Frenchman has cited the different meanings as given by ancient writers of the word *Zarathushtra* (the Zend for

I shall not repeat what I have said of the native country of Zoroaster, in my first *Memoire** on the ancient languages of Persia. It is most frequently the lot of extraordinary men, to leave to posterity only a vague sound of their names. Fortunate even, if the empty title of their first splendour is not swept off by barbarity which succeeds them, or by those even who trust to perpetuating their glory. These names pass through a hundred foreign tongues, whose different pronunciations make the original disappear. At the end of a few centuries, the noise, which their actions or their books continually make, leads historians to adorn with their names those who are distinguished in the same manner, or to identify them with some personages more ancient than those whom they resemble. Thus new sources of difficulties and even errors arise, when one wishes to determine the time in which they flourished.

The same remarks apply to the places which have given them birth—the clouds which it is nearly impossible to disperse. Twenty different places claim the honour of his birth. Were Zoroaster, for example, to revisit the earth, would he recognise the portraits which people have given of him?

* * * * * †

Zoroaster.) According to his opinion *Zarathushtra* literally means "the golden or bright star." But the true sense of this very ancient word has not as yet been settled by oriental scholars. For further particulars, see Mr. K. R. Cama's *Zertosht Námeh*, pp. 17–28.—*Translator*.

* Mem. de l'Acad. des Bel.—Lett. T. XXXI. pag. 370 et suiv.

† Mon. Anquetil here gives an account, on the authority of the Zertosht Námeh, of a strange dream seen by Zoroaster's mother Dogdo during the 6th month of her pregnancy, and the interpretation thereof by a well-known astrologer of the time, which was that

A young man such as Zoroaster, little concerned about the happiness of this world and the pleasures of his age, could not relish the society of the inhabitants of Urmi,* who, for the most part, were given up to magicians. The study of wisdom formed his happiness at the age of 20 or 25. Being within reach of consultation with the Chaldean sages, there was no doubt then that he took lessons from them; and the sublime learning, which he drew from their writings, was the germ of the truths which he afterwards announced to the whole of Persia.

* * * * *

If from all that has been ascribed to him we deduct the marvels inseparable from the position which he was going to enjoy, and the predictions made by him which relate

---

her son would be a great prophet, and that he would destroy Devs, magicians and evil doers on the surface of the earth, and that he would preach morality to men and show them the path to heaven.—*Translator*.

* Mon. Anquetil believes that Zoroaster was born about 550B.C. in Urmi (a town in Azerbeján). But it is not so. According to the most recent researches, the prophet was born in the city of Rai (Zend *Ragha*) in Irân Vej about 2300 B. C. The late lamented Dr. Haug, at the end of his "Lecture on an original speech of Zoroaster (Yaçna 45), with remarks on his age," writes as follows :—

" * * According to this investigation we cannot assign to Zarathustra Spitama a later date than about 2300 B. C. Thus he lived not only before Moses, but even, perhaps, before Abraham. If we consider the early age in which he lived, it is not surprising that the high and lofty ideas which he proclaimed were early misunderstood and misinterpreted; for he stood far above his age. So he was the first prophet of truth who appeared in the world, and kindled a fire which thousands of years could not entirely extinguish."

From the 19th Fargard of the Vendidad we find that his father Poroshasp's house was situated on the bank of the Derjic (Zend *Darĕja*), a river which flowed from the Zabâr Mountain into Irân Vej. For further particulars see Mr. K. R. Cama's *Zertoshti Abhyâs*, pp. 11–15 and pp. 69–74, and *Zertosht Nâmeh*, pp. 32–41.—*Translator*.

to Aderbád, and which have been very lately added, it presents nothing which does not correspond with what the ancient writers inform us of this Legislator. According to Parsi books, Zoroaster consulted Ormazd on the mountains; and we are assured, from the time of Dion Chrysostome, that on a principle of love for wisdom and justice, this Legislator withdrew himself from the intercourse of men and lived alone on the mountain.

The mountain to which Zoroaster retired was probably that of which Eubulus has spoken. Zoroaster, according to this writer, cited by Porphyre, was the first who had consecrated in the neighbouring mountains of Persia (Alborj or the mountains of Balkh) a cavern to Mithra,* the King and the Father of all that exists. He wished that that cavern would represent him as the image of the world, created by Mithra, and that the things which it contained, put at fixed distances from one another, would represent the symbols or figures of the elements and climates.

This spectacle was very proper to remind him of the brilliancy of His system, by putting before his eyes the constant order of the universe, its different parts, the elements of which it is composed—this whole harmony protected by Mithra, companion of the sun and the moon.

It is probably from these symbols that the Parsis, according to Celse, represent, in the ceremonies of Mithra, the double movement of stars, fixed stars and planets, as well as the passage of souls through these celestial bodies. In order to mark some of the properties of the planets, they

---

* For the explanation of this, see Mr. K. R. Cama's "Discourse on the Mithraic worship, and the rites and mysteries connected with it."—*Translator.*

erect a ladder; along the length thereof there are seven gates, and an eighth one at the top. The first of lead denoted Saturn; the second of tin, Venus; the third of copper, Jupiter; the fourth of iron, Mercury; the fifth of divers metals, Mars; the sixth of silver, the moon; and the seventh of gold, the sun. The Parsis actually recognise different Heavens in which the souls of the dead enjoy, up to the Resurrection, felicity proportionate to the sanctity of their past life; that of the sun (Khorshed-pâe) is the most exalted. Above it is the Garothmân, the abode of Ormazd and other celestial spirits, and which corresponds to the eighth gate to which Celse has alluded.*

We have yet to give an account of the time which Zoroaster passed on the mountains and of the ten years which preceded it, of which we read in Pliny: it is related, says this naturalist, that Zoroaster passed twenty years in desert places, having for nourishment cheese only made in a manner not liable to be spoiled during all that time.

* * * * * †

---

* See Mr. K. R. Cama's "Discourse on the Mithraic worship, &c." pp. 23-25.—*Translator.*

† Mon. Anquetil here gives a narrative of the miracles wrought by Zoroaster at the court of King Gushtasp. In reference to these he says:—"I thought it better to omit them. Two considerations have made me change my opinion. 1.—The ancient writers, Greek as well as Latin, little interested in extolling Zoroaster, have related some of his miracles. 2.—These facts, cited at divers times by writers belonging to nationalities and religions absolutely different, acquaint us with the genius of a large portion of mankind. Besides, a man like Zoroaster ought neither to be born, nor to live nor die like ordinary mortals. One would better judge Zoroaster by omitting the miracles which (in the works I have cited, viz., the Zertosht Nâmeh and the Changraghâch Nâmeh) accompany all his acts than trust to criticism, which would do me honor without satisfying the curiosity of the reader with regard to what I would have omitted."

The zeal of King Gushtasp fully supported the enthusiasm of his Prophet. He evinced it at first by elevating Atash-Gâhs (Fire-temples). He consecrated one (Atash-Gâh) to the Fire *Farpa,* honoured by Jamsheed on the Kharesom mountain, near Kasbin in Verjamkerd; another to the Fire *Goshasp* to which Kaikhosru had elevated an Atash-Gâh on the Asnévand mountain in Azerbeján; a third to the Fire *Bourzin-Méher* and to the Fire *Béherám,* which he formed out of different fires put together. He appointed Mobeds and Dustoors everywhere.

There was in Cashmere, a village of Khorásán, a celebrated Atash-Gâh, near the gate of which Zoroaster planted a cypress and engraved on the bark of its trunk the fact of King Gushtasp having embraced his religion. Many years after, this cypress having grown great and thickly overspread with branches, a palace 40 cubits in height was built over it in the form of a square. It contained two halls, the roof of which was of gold, the floor of silver and the walls of amber, adorned with precious stones. Likenesses of Jamsheed and Feridoon were sculptured therein. Gushtasp retired to that palace to go thence to heaven when his hour came.

This prince despatched afterwards his messengers to the extremities of his empire, and desired the governors to

---

As for the Zertosht Námeh, a poetical work written in Persian, the learned Frenchman gives the following note :—

"Zertosht Behrám, author of the Zertosht Námeh, informs us in the last chapter of that work, that he has translated it from the Pehlvi text, read out to him by a Mobed proficient in that language; and in the same chapter where he states his name, he says that he wrote the Zertosht Námeh in the year of Yezdegird 647, corresponding with the Christian year 1278. If there be no error in the text, the Zertosht Námeh (in Persian) would be 500 years old. I have followed the opinion of the Dustoors of India."

come on foot to visit the cypress, to pay attention to Zoroaster and to abandon the worship of the idols of Touran and China.

* * * * * †

Then not content with seeing his religion carried to the confines of Hindostan, and received in many provinces of Persia, Zoroaster wished the Chaldeans themselves, from whom he had received his early lessons, to submit to his religion.

At Babylon, Pythagoras was initiated into his mysteries in the same manner as the Brahmins of India; and no doubt, the example of this philosopher was followed by a great number of inhabitants and foreigners, especially by the Medes who had settled in that town.

The Legislator of Persia had also accompanied Gushtasp to Istakhr; and he, who called himself messenger from God sent to the whole world, had visited at least the regions of Serman, Saenan and Dahou,* in which were the Fravashis of the pure whose eulogy he sings.

His different journeys, his miracles, such as the recovery of Lohrâsp at Balkh, the composition of several works and the exercise of the office of the first Dustoor of Irán

† Here the learned Frenchman gives an account of the Changraghâch Námeh, a small poetical work written in Persian about 300 years ago. Changraghâch, a very learned and accomplished Brahmin metaphysician, was called from India by King Gushtasp at his court to discuss with Zoroaster the doctrines of the religion founded by him. Tradition says that the discussion, which was conducted for several days in the presence of a very learned assembly, resulted in the conviction of the Hindoo philosopher of the morality preached by Zoroaster.—*Translator.*

* In Zend *çairima, çâini* and *dâhi,* see Farvardin Yasht, 31st chapter.—*Translator.*

—these are all that we know of the doings of Zoroaster during the twenty years which followed his conference with Changraghâch, the Hindoo philosopher.

* * * * *

The English authors of Universal History find nothing in Zoroaster, which presents either enthusiasm, sorcery or imposture. The glorious testimonies which the ancient writers bear to him, his sublime doctrine, his pure ethics, his learning—all these conspire to show that he was a philosopher animated with a love of wisdom. "The Magi," they say, "clad in coarse garments and living with the greatest frugality, resemble rather the precursors of Messiah "than the courtiers who flatter the pride of kings and who "make use of their religion for their particular views."

What these disinterested writers speak of the cave of Zoroaster appears to me to be very just. Is it not ridiculous to impute crime to a philosopher and speculator, because he chose, remote from the tumult of men, the silence of the retreat of a cave, to contemplate the sublime truths of nature?

Moreover, I agree with these learned historians that it is incredible that Zoroaster could have been inspired by the father of falsehood, since his doctrine was not calculated to countenance the views of the Demon, who, obeying the decision of the Eternal Wisdom, does not guard against the destruction of his own empire.

It is true that I shall accuse him neither of sorcery nor magic, because I regard all the prodigies which his life makes mention of as invented by his disciples; and I observe at the same time that the supposition, partly at least, is anterior to Mahomedanism, and even to the Sassanian dynasty, since Pliny and Solon give an account of some of them.

If, however, we understand by magic the invocation of good spirits, which has for its special object the good of men, or rather the recital of certain formulæ to which God Himself is supposed to have attached some special grace—I willingly admit that Zoroaster has exercised it. It appears from the list of treatises which the Ravâets attribute to him, that many of his works related to the art of working miracles. He positively says that the most perfect cure is that which is effected by the divine Word. Zend books show us a Legislator in communion with the Supreme Being, and thereby master of good and evil. The Magi, his disciples, employed for curing maladies means different from natural ones. But the magic, taken in *this* sense, presents nothing which wounds the attributes of the Deity or degrades the creature: it is only a question of not extending it too far; so I do not believe that we can make a crime of it on the part of Zoroaster.

This Legislator probably passed his youth in contemplating the most sublime truths: his genius called to his aid all the materials for meditation. Retired to the mountains, he had learnt to despise the riches and conveniences of life. Milk was the only nourishment which he always took, if what has been said since the time of Plutarch be true. A right sense dictated to him the purest morality. He saw that sin against nature depopulated the earth; that the doctrine regarding the two principles existing by themselves, and that of the two lives, appeared to deprive some of the most atrocious crimes of their proper punishment; that the intercourse with the magicians multiplied them, supported ignorance and idleness, and rendered arts and agriculture useless, by perpetuating the idea, which the people had, that evil spirits could give the people all which they stood in need of. How to reclaim men, how to check them in their slippery path of passions, if it be not by religion? At first, Zoroaster collects what his genius suggests to him, and all the learning which he had acquired in his travels, such as astronomy, agriculture, natural history, &c. This new knowledge rendered the invocation of the aid of evil spirits useless: men enriched with their own works, and having witnessed the order which reigns in Nature, went up easily to their Creator and became more qualified to receive the truths which this Legislator wished to impart to them.

In a journey which Zoroaster makes to Chaldea or to the north of Iran, he is instructed in the dogmas which are attributed to the famous Hom. Transported with these which show him the origin of mankind and the cause of evils which overpower them, he studies them attentively, and believes himself instructed by Hom himself. Perhaps some singular event, which happened at the time of his birth, persuaded him that, descended from the blood of the ancient Kings of Persia, he was destined to give laws to his native country.

The new prophet consequently takes his way to Balkh, and explains there his law. At Babylon, the seat of the sages of the East, he expounds his ethics, developes his system, and begets conviction by his teachings.

We ought not then to look on Zoroaster as a mere philosopher, who writes out coldly the system of the universe, and composes a body of doctrines which his shrewd disciples undertake to sustain by argument. The ancient Legislators have not followed this course.

* * * *

Zoroaster traces this religion which he seeks to establish as anterior to Jamsheed. Hom, according to him, at first proclaimed it on the mountains. The Parsi Legislator knew that the people reasoned little, and that they were more impressed with the outward show of ceremonies, and by the confident tone of him who proposed them rather than with the abstract spirit of religion: so he gives himself out boldly as the Minister of God. He presents his books as the Word of Ormazd, the most minute practices as emanating from the throne of the Supreme Being.

CEREMONIAL AND ETHICAL SYSTEM

OF

ZEND AND PEHLVI BOOKS,

CONSIDERED BY ITSELF, AND IN RELATION TO THE THEOLOGICAL SYSTEM OF THE SAME BOOKS.

I. The theological dogmas, on which the religion of the Parsis is founded, are so dispersed in their ancient books, and appear in such a form that even those who are most familiar with the works of the Orientals will find them undoubtedly strange. Without wishing to anticipate the judgment which may be formed of these dogmas, and of the manner in which they are presented, I venture to place them here in the proper order of their relations to one another. These dogmas form a system, of which the principal points, as I have shown in a work already mentioned,[1] are the following:—

(1.) Time without Bounds, the First Principle[2] which

[1] Exposition du systême théologique des Perses, tiré des Livres Zends, Pehlvis et Parsis.

[2] The theory that *Zarvâna Akarana* (Time without Bounds) is the First Cause which created Ormazd and Ahriman is entirely dissonant from the original spirit of the Zoroastrian religion. Scholars like Drs. Spiegel and Haug have convincingly shown that the First Cause which created the whole universe is *Ahura-Mazda* (the name of God throughout the Zend-Avesta). For full particulars see Dr. Spiegel's discourse on Zarvâna Akarana in Zeitschr. der Deutsch morgenl. Ges. V., and Dr. Haug's "Essays on the sacred language, writings and religion of the Parsis," pp. 20-21 and pp. 263-264.—*Translator.*

creates the first light, the first water, the original fire, Ormazd and Ahriman; the Word which preceded all created beings, and by which the production of these beings was effected: Ormazd and Ahriman, secondary principles, active and productive, the first, good by essence and the source of all good; the second, corrupt and the cause of all evil.

(2.) The duration of the time with bounds fixed, by Time without Bounds, to twelve thousand years, and divided between Ormazd and Ahriman; the war of these two principles and the victories which they achieve alternately over each other, terminating in the triumph of Ormazd.[3]

(3.) The Farohers, or first models of beings, which Ormazd creates to fight against Ahriman, and of which the most precious to his eyes are the Faroher of the Religion, and that of Zoroaster, charged to re-establish, by publishing that Religion, the glory of the Master of Nature: the successive production in favour of these Farohers, of different beings, spiritual and corporeal, who form the world of Ormazd, and particularly of Irán Vej—a world which Ahriman opposes with evil spirits, and a world wicked and corrupt as himself.

(4.) The distribution of the universe of which all the parts are submitted to the action of the good spirits, created by Ormazd, and which resort to this Principle of Good;

---

[3] Ormazd and Ahriman are not, as Mon. Anquetil supposes them to be, the two rivals acting in opposition to each other. The theology of Zoroaster is not based on these two principles, but on monotheism. Ormazd is the *sole* Creator and Master of the whole universe. This fact is easily ascertained from the Gâthâs. For full particulars see Dr. Haug's "Essays on the sacred language, writings and religion of the Parsis," pp. 256–259; Dr. Haug's "Lecture on an original speech of Zoroaster (Yaçna 45), with remarks on his age," pp. 6–8; Mr. K. R. Cama's Zertosht Námeh, pp. 106–120; Mr. K. R. Cama's "Discourse on Zoroastrians and Freemasonry," pp. 20–22.—*Translator.*

these form a line of agents who ascend to Time without Bounds:[4] the creation of the first Bull, from which the whole human race, animals and vegetables, are sprung; that of Gayomard, of the soul, pure and immortal, of man created just and free; the sin of Mashya and Mashyâni, parents of human kind: the cause of the mixture of good and evil which appears in Nature—a mixture which results from the contrary actions of the people of Ormazd and those of Ahriman.[5]

(5.) Lastly, the deliverance of man unto death, the abode destined for the just, and that which is reserved for the sinful; the Resurrection[6] of bodies preceded by the conversion of the whole world to the Law of Zoroaster, and followed, according to the order established by Time without Bounds, by new punishments which ought to open to the sinner the gates of Garothmân; sinners purified by the punishments of Hell, by the fire of metals and happy afterwards eternally along with the just; the general re-establishment of Nature, hell itself renewed; the world of Ahriman destroyed, and Ormazd on one side with his seven primary Izeds (angels); Ahriman, on the other, accompanied with his seven primary Devs (devils), offering together a sacrifice of praise to the First Being.[5]

It is on this system, the harmony of which few of the Dustoors conceive properly, for the most instructed even

---

[4] In refutation of this opinion of the author see p. 65, note 1. —*Translator.*

[5] In refutation of this opinion of the author see p. 66, note 3. —*Translator.*

[6] In order to have an idea of the Zoroastrian doctrine for the Resurrection the reader's attention is directed to Dr. Haug's "Essays on the sacred language, writings and religion of the Parsis," pp. 6–7, 196, 266–268.—*Translator.*

understand it superficially only—without searching for its allegorical sense to which the Parsi works give no clue—it is on this system that the religion of the Parsis rests. The whole may properly be reduced to two points.

The first, to begin with, is to recognise and adore the Master of all that is good, the Principle of Justice, Ormazd,[7] according to the religious worship which He has prescribed, with purity of thought, of word and of action—a purity which should always be accompanied with the indication and preservation of the purity of the body, in conformity with the Law of Zoroaster. In the second place, to revere with thankfulness the Intelligences (or heavenly spirits) whom Ormazd has charged with the care of Nature,[8] to take up as models for action their attributes, to take for guidance in conduct the harmony which reigns between the different parts of the universe, and generally to adore Ormazd in all that He has created.

The second point of the religion of the Parsis consists in detesting Ahriman,[9] the author of every evil, moral and physical, his productions and his works; and to contribute as much as possible to extol the glory of Ormazd, by enfeebling the tyranny which the Evil Principle exercises over the world created by the Good Principle.

It is with these two points that the prayers, the religious practices, the civil usages and the precepts of morality, which the Zend and Pehlvi books present, are connected;

---

[7] See Yaçna, chapter 1, para. 1, ; chapter 16, para. 1.—*Tr.*

[8] See Zamyâd Yasht, chapter 3; Yaçna, chapter 14, para 1; Yaçna, chapter 16, paras. 3–6.—*Translator.*

[9] See Vendidad, Fargard 10, para. 5; Khorshed Nyâesh, para. 2; Yaçna, chapter 12, paras. 4–7.—*Translator.*

and these different subjects originate, as we shall see, with the theological speculations of the Legislator of the Parsis.

II. At first, as the religion, so to speak, is the embodiment of the manifestation of the First Word, which has created the world, so the reading of the books which contain it is an homage rendered to that Word, and becomes thereby of an absolute necessity. Moreover, these books, when read in a proper spirit, ought to have here an efficacy which corresponds in some measure with that which the primitive Word has operated on the origin of beings.

Prayer is one of the duties most recommended, because man, being the butt of the continual attacks of Ahriman, has need of the succour which it (the prayer) procures, and because it gives occasion to the Intelligences (or heavenly spirits) to whom it is addressed, to perform the functions for which they are created.

The priest prays for himself, for all Parsis, and in particular, as from the time of Herodotus, for the king whom Ormazd has placed over His people; and in order to give greater efficacy to them, he unites his prayers with those of all Parsis, of all the souls acceptable to Ormazd, which *have* existed or which *are* to exist up to the day of the Resurrection. He declares likewise that he takes part in all the good works of the just and that he joins his action to theirs. This communion of prayers and actions appears in all the formulæ, in all the offices which compose the liturgical books of the Parsis, and is very proper for entertaining the spirit of peace and union which ought to characterise a people, who profess to adore the Author of every good.

The Parsis commence their prayers with a sincere

avowal of the sins they have committed, and address them to Time without Bounds,[10] to Ormazd, to the numerous body created in the beginning, that is to say, the Amshâspands and other celestial spirits who take care of the different elements composing the universe. The prayers offered to them relate to their respective functions; and if they are addressed to the stars, they must be done at the time when they are visible. The Parsis pray to the sun during day-time, and to the moon both by day and night. Mithra is praised because he fights against the creatures of Ahriman, and because he renders the fields fruitful; one spirit presides over the waters and another protects the soul ready to depart from the body.

Next to the celestial spirits, the entire Nature, exposed to our eyes, merits, say the Parsis, our adoration, because she takes her birth from Ormazd. She does not contain any species of being, of which the Zend and Pehlvi books make no mention. Some of these are employed to celebrate others: wood and fragrant drugs enter into the offerings made to the elements, the stars, &c.

Among the number of the elements is the material fire which represents, though imperfectly, the original fire, which animates all beings, forms their connections and works since the commencement. The original fire was, and still is, manifested on earth, in trees, animals and man, in different manners which are called sons of Ormazd, either because there exists a more intimate relation of Nature between Ormazd and fire[11] than between other creatures and Him from whom they received their existence; or because that

---

[10] In refutation of this opinion of the author see p. 65, note 1. —*Translator*.

[11] See Mr. K. R. Cama's "Discourse on the Mithraic worship, &c.," p. 12, note 1.—*Translator*.

element is, like Ormazd, the most universal principle of life and motion.[12]

It was therefore natural that Zoroaster, regarding fire as the *purest* symbol of the ever-working Divinity, recommended its special worship: and as, of all the elements, fire is the only one which would not be visible unless it was lighted, this Legislator ordained to have altars (or Fire-temples) raised, on which it might be preserved.

Hence, fire became the most ordinary and striking object of the worship of the Parsis. Hence, the remark of Strabo that to whatever Ized the Persians might give offerings, they first invoked fire. We see in fact Cyrus sacrificing first to Vesta (fire) and afterwards to Jupiter; and the Parsis recite the greatest number of their prayers in the presence of that element: the Nyâesh of fire is celebrated day and night, and it is ordained to the Mobed to put wood and fragrant drugs on fire during the five Géhs (watches) of the day.[13]

One ought not, after this, to be surprised that he who defiles that element is punished severely. It is prohibited, as from the time of Clitarchus, cited by Diogenes Laertius, to burn dead bodies,[14] because they are impure. The same reason leads the Parsis to remove corpses away from the fire.[15]

---

[12] See Yaçna, chapter 17, para. 11; chapter 36.—*Translator.*

[13] The five Géhs or Gâhs are :—1, Ushahina; 2, Hâvani; 3, Rapithwina; 4, Uzayêirina; 5, Aiwiçruthrema. For the explanation of these Zend terms see *Zertoshti Abhyâs,* No. 7, pp. 371–376.—*Translator.*

[14] See Vendidad, Fargard 1, para. 17; Fargard 7, paras. 25–26. —*Translator.*

[15] See Vendidad, Fargard 8, paras. 73–74.—*Translator.*

The detail of ceremonies necessary to perform for restoring fire to its first state, when it has been defiled,[16] marks its extreme purity. The sap, while nourishing the tree, makes it grow, changes in some sort its body, and thus purifies it when it has been defiled. Such is not the case with fire: and now to supply the place of the successive alteration which Nature produces in the vegetable kingdom, the Zend books ordain that the fire in which a dead body had been burnt should, in some sort, be made to pass through nine different fires, before it could be used for the purpose of veneration by the Parsis in the Dâd-gâh.[17] The Atash-Behrám, protector of countries and states, is the extract of 1001 fires taken from 15[18] different kinds of fire.

But the worship, which the Parsis render to fire, as well as to other creatures, is subordinate to that of Ormazd, whose praise commences and finishes all offices of religion.

These offices cannot please the Divinity unless they flow from a pure heart; and purity of heart supposes purity of body. The first is the rule of thoughts, words and deeds: it is accompanied with the knowledge of the religion, and sustained by good works done with conscious intelligence. The priest, who tends to this purity, ought to do good like the first of the Amshâspands: he must be learned, true in his words, grown-up and full of intelligence:[19] these are in

---

[16] See Vendidad, Fargard 8, paras. 73–78.—*Translator*.

[17] Dâd-gâh (the Zend equivalent for which is *dâityo-gâtu*) literally means a proper place; (see Vendidad, Fargard 13, paras. 17, 18, 19; Fargard 8, paras. 81–96); here it means the proper place for the fire.—*Translator*.

[18] Not fifteen, but sixteen different kinds of fire (see Vendidad, Fargard 8, paras. 81–96.—*Translator*.

[19] See Vendidad, Farg. 9, para. 2; Farg. 13, para. 45; Farg. 18, paras. 1–6.—*Translator*.

fact the qualities with which Zoroaster presents himself before the Supreme Being. Purity of body is necessary, because it arrests the efforts of evil spirits, and obliging the Parsi to a continual circumspection, it renders him more attentive to the practices of the religion, the principal object of which is to annihilate the empire of Ahriman.[20]

The obligation to preserve purity of body has given birth to a number of usages in the religion of the Parsis. For instance, as the offspring of Mashya and Mashyâni, man is born impure, because the body of his first parents came from that of Gayomard[21] which Ahriman had defiled; and ablutions can well purify the outside of the body, but not the inside: consequently what comes out from it is impure. Hence, the obligation, when one prays or eats to have the Padân[22] on the face in order to check the saliva from defiling the things on which it would fall. Hence, as from the time of Herodotus, the prohibition against throwing into water anything which comes from the body of man. During prayers, meals and the performance of natural functions it is prohibited to speak; one can emit inarticulate sounds almost as dumb persons do: this is what is called speaking in *Bâj*. The same principle obliges the Parsis to remove from inhabited places, as was the usage among them from the time of Herodotus, lepers[23] and those who are afflicted with contagious diseases. These evils come from Ahriman. The same principle obliges them to render to

---

[20] See Vendidad, Farg. 19, paras. 5–10. Arshashang Yasht, paras. 19–20.—*Translator*.

[21] See Farvardin Yasht, paras. 87 and 145; Yaçna, chapter 26, para. 10.—*Translator*.

[22] This is an erroneous impression. No layman or priest ever puts on Padân whilst taking his meals.—*Translator*.

[23] See Vendidad, Farg. 2, paras. 29 and 37.—*Translator*.

the dead the last ceremonies, the ceremonies which they use in driving away the Devs who attack dead bodies and who defile all those who surround them.

But the feebleness of man not permitting him to keep so scrupulous an attention upon himself, it was necessary to give means to recover that purity, when one should have lost it: such is the object of the purifications prescribed by the law of Zoroaster. Water, which forms the principal material[24] for these, drives away all evils and gives every good; and the juice of the *Hom* is in this life an element of strength against the attacks of evil spirits.[25]

Even involuntary pollutions can only be washed away by purifications. Hence arises the necessity of ablutions before and after natural functions;[26] the injunction to wash the new-born infant; the purifications ordained to females after child-birth, menses,[27] &c. But when it is impossible for one, who is defiled, to practise what the religion prescribes on this matter, a sincere repentance, and prayers offered with an humble and pure heart, supply the place of outward ceremonies: and, if the punishment of death is adjudged for certain voluntary legal impurities, it is because man, to whom the law is given, being a free agent and master consequently of his own actions, is the real cause of his own suffering; he is the follower of a religion, in which everything is directed against the author of evil: that is

---

[24] See Vendidad, Farg. 8, paras. 40–72; Farg. 9, para. 31; Farg. 19, para. 22.—*Translator.*

[25] See Yaçna, chapters 9–10.—*Translator.*

[26] There are no ablutions practised by the Parsis *before* natural functions.—*Translator.*

[27] See Vendidad, Farg. 5, paras. 45–56; Farg. 16, paras. 1–12.—*Translator.*

to say, a Parsi ought to know that errors of this kind, by thus tending to the superiority of Ahriman and the humiliation (so to speak) of Ormazd,[28] become capital crimes. On the other hand, the Dustoors believe, that, by exercise of this severity, they render the greatest service to the transgressor: by suffering this punishment, the man exhausts on himself the malice of the impure spirits, triumphs over them, and becomes eligible, by his submission, to be admitted into the abode of the happy.

Up to here we have seen Zoroaster prescribing observances, connected with his theological ideas and calculated to render man worthy of the favours of Ormazd; but this Legislator, in the enforcement of such precepts, had still another aim in view, viz., the general good of Nature.[29] These observances ought then to be directed, as his ethics, towards the particular advantage of the Parsi; and then these would be so many laws of police, often relative to the country which the Parsi Legislator inhabited. I stop to notice some of these observances.

In including venomous creatures, reptiles, insects, voracious and ferocious animals, such as the wolf, in the number of the productions of Ahriman, Zoroaster has likewise had in view the special good of the Parsis: hence he enjoins them to destroy these animals,[30] and interdicts them at the same time from the use of their flesh which is naturally very unwholesome.

Of all known religions, that of the Parsis is perhaps

---

[28] In refutation of this opinion of the author see p. 66, note 3. —*Translator.*

[29] See Mr. K. R. Cama's *Zertosht Nâmeh*, pp. 216–218.—*Tr.*

[30] See Vend. Farg. 14, paras. 5–6; Farg. 16, para. 12; Farg. 18, para. 73.—*Tr.*

the only one in which fasting is neither considered meritorious nor permitted.[31] The Parsi, on the contrary, believes to honour Ormazd by nourishing himself well: because the body, when fresh and vigorous, renders the soul more powerful to resist the attacks of evil spirits; and because man, feeling himself less in need of food, reads the Word with greater attention and has more courage to perform good actions ; consequently, several celestial spirits are charged specially to watch over the comforts of man : Râmashné Khârom, Khordâd and Amerdâd give him abundance and pleasures, and it is the last-mentioned Ized who produces taste in fruits—the savour which contributes to their employment for the purpose for which Ormazd has created them.

Purifications, in warm or moist and marshy countries, contribute to health ; and such is the climate of Persia : the provinces of Ghilân and Mâzenderân, situated to the north, are full of unhealthy exhalations, while a burning sun parches the provinces towards the south. And, if the most efficacious purifications are at first made with the ox's urine, it is on account of the virtue which the cure of Jamsheed has caused to be observed in that liquid, or rather, because the bull gave birth to the human race. But the purifications are always concluded with water, preceded by dry earth which must dry up the last drop of the urine, which, so to speak, becomes impregnated with all that is nauseous in the impurities.[32]

Besides, whatever may have been the motive of this institution, it always follows from this, that the Parsi is

---

[31] See Vend. Farg. 3, para. 33; and Mr. K. R. Cama's *Zertosht Nâmeh*, pp. 216–228.—*Tr.*

[32] See Vend. Farg. 8, paras. 35–72 ; Farg. 9, paras. 14–36.—*Tr.*

obliged to have an ox and a cow in his house. It is still necessary, on account of the *Sag-did,* that he must have at least a dog; and the qualities of the cock, who is the *Vizir* of Serosh on earth, and defends men against the snares of evil spirits,[33] put him to the necessity of having that animal also. Now these three animals are the most necessary to a Parsi; they supply likewise all his wants: the ox serves for tillage[34] and for drawing carts, the cow supplies milk,[35] the dog watches flocks and herds by day, and the house by night;[36] the hen lays eggs; at the crowing of the cock, at day-break, prayers, the labours of the field, and other occupations of men commence.[37]

The place to which dead bodies are conveyed ought to be on mountains,[38] or at a fixed distance from main roads, cultivated fields, and inhabited places; and we know that independent of the legal impurity which the portions of the dead body, carried away by carnivorous animals, could produce, the atmosphere near these sorts of places is usually very unhealthy.

Even the feasts of the Parsis, at least the most solemn of them, appear only to recall the grand events of Nature, which personally interest the Parsi, or to mark the approach of different seasons. I have spoken of the *Gáhámbárs,*[39] which

---

[33] See Vend. Farg. 18, paras. 14–16.—*Tr.*

[34] See Vend. Farg. 3, paras. 23–32.—*Tr.*

[35] See Vend. Farg. 5, para. 52; Farg. 7, para. 77.—*Tr.*

[36] See Vend. Farg. 13, paras. 10–11, 17–18, 39–40, 45–46, 49. —*Translator.*

[37] See Vend. Farg. 18, paras. 22–24.—*Tr.*

[38] See Vend. Farg. 6, paras. 44–45.—*Tr.*

[39] For the explanation of this term see Mr. K. R. Cama's *Zertoshti Abhyâs,* No. 7, pp. 403–412 and pp. 433–453, and No. 11.—*Translator.*

are celebrated at different periods of the year, and which correspond to those in which Ormazd, at the beginning of the world, created the beings that compose the universe. Next to these feasts, the most solemn are the *Nowroz* and the *Méhergân*.[40] The first of these two, since the time of Zoroaster, has corresponded to the Spring, and the second, which comes six months after, to the Autumn—the seasons in which the birth of Nature and her fecundity announce the triumph of Ormazd. It was probably for the same reason that marriages among the Parsis are celebrated at the Vernal Equinox.

Finally, the ceremonies attendant on funerals, the prayers recited at the time, those which precede and those which follow—all these tend to show the Parsis that, to the righteous alone death is the passage to a happy life; but to the wicked the commencement of punishments which expiate their sins, and from which the prayers of the living can deliver them. The love which they bear for their kinsmen, their masters and their friends, who are separated from them only for a time, is manifested by these prayers. Their religion still goes further; when a man has committed certain faults, it ordains to his kinsmen and friends, after his death, to perform pious deeds, and give alms in expiation of those crimes. These actions shorten the period which the deceased sinner has to pass in hell.[41]

---

[40] See Mr. K. R. Cama's "Discourse on the Mithraic worship, &c." pp. 7–8; pp. 20–21.—*Translator.*

[41] From the Zend books we find that a man, after his death, gets a higher or a lower place in the next world according to his good or bad actions whilst living. Whatever good a man does during his life-time becomes of great use to him in after life. The doctrine that prayers and religious rites for the sinful dead tend in some measure to mitigate their punishment in the next world is to be found in later works written on the Zoroastrian religion. For particulars see Vendidad, Fargard 19, paras. 27–33; Ardibéhesht Yasht, para. 4; Hâ-

It was worthy of him who regarded created Intelligences as the Ministers of the Eternal, and the death of man as a temporary separation of the parts which make up his being, and which ought one day to be re-united,—it was worthy of him, who, as I shall show further below, considered the essence of his religion to consist in what Nature herself inspires, and connects with the purest and most tender pleasure, viz., the respect of the creature for his Creator, and for all that He has made, the reciprocal affection of parents and children, of husband and wife, of king and his subjects, of master and pupil,—it was worthy of such a Legislator to break off the barrier which death but too frequently puts to affections so lawful, and to render thereby the bond with which he wished to unite all parts of the universe as his eternal principle.

III. The ethics of Zoroaster, as well as the practices which it prescribes, has for its end the glory of Ormazd, the general good of Nature, of society in general, and of the Parsi in particular. I understand by ethics the precepts relative to the good and the evil of actions; for the Parsis know not indifferent works: a thing is either agreeable to Ormazd or to Ahriman, as Nature is divided between these two Principles.[42]

In their religion there is no place either for sanctity *purely speculative,* or for those spiritualities, which, under pretext of uniting more the creature with the Creator, authorise idleness and gratify self-love. Everything in the religion of the Parsi is in *actions,* and ought to conspire to

---

dokht Yasht; Mr. K. R. Cama's "Discourse on Zoroastrians and Freemasonry," pp. 7–9.—*Translator.*

[42] In refutation of this opinion of the author see p. 66, note 3. —*Translator.*

promote the good of the human race. Zoroaster himself shows the example: he demands immortality; Ormazd answers him that if He would accord that grace, the Resurrection would not arrive, and the Legislator consents to die.

The ethics of Zoroaster may be divided into two parts. The first includes the duties of the creature towards the Creator. These are expressed in a few words, and comprehend all the duties of man. There are, says Ormazd, three rules of conduct. These are *purity of thought, purity of word and purity of deed*;[43] and he who possesses this purity ought to exert himself to cultivate it. The Parsi Dustoors add that a good work should not be put off to another day. In these peculiarities we recognise the justice, of which the Magi spoke as reported by Clitarque. Without these essentials, all offerings and preparations enjoined by the religion are useless.

The second part of the ethics of Zoroaster relates to society and may be called his sociology. This Legislator having found the Parsis divided into four classes, as from the time of King Jamsheed,[44] confirms such divisions. He as-

[43] Do not turn yourselves away from the three best things, viz., good thoughts, good words and good deeds. Turn yourselves away from the three worst things, viz., evil thoughts, evil words and evil deeds (see Vendidad, Fargard 18, paras. 17 and 25). All good thoughts, good words and good deeds lead to Paradise; all evil thoughts, evil words and evil deeds lead to hell (see the prayer *Viçpa-Humata*). I praise the well-thought, well-spoken, well-performed thoughts, words and deeds. I lay hold on all good thoughts, good words and good deeds. I abandon all evil thoughts, evil words and evil deeds. (See Yaçna, chapter 11, para. 17).—*Translator.*

[44] The four classes are as follow :—1, priests (Zend *Athravan*); 2, kings and warriors (Zend *Rathaestar*); 3, agriculturists (Zend *Vâctrya Fshuyant*); 4, artisans (Zend *Hûiti*) (see Yaçna, chapter XIX, para. 17). In the Shâh-Nâmeh we read to the same effect, viz., that King Jamsheed divided his subjects into four classes, called respec-

signs particular duties to these classes; he even enters into the details of the instruments or the utensils necessary to each profession:[45] and as he does not lose sight of the good of man, he insists on the possession of those qualities which those, to whose care life and body are particularly entrusted, ought to have. Let the physician, says he, improve and render himself more skilful:[46] his business is to give health. The sanctity, learning and other qualities which this Legislator demands from the priest,[47] correspond perfectly with the description which the ancient writers give us of the Magi.

Afterwards, always occupied with the form of government which Ormazd has established in Nature, Zoroaster enjoins that professions should have their chiefs, and that he, who is elevated to that dignity, must have eminently the qualifications of the profession to which he belongs. Thus the chief of priests ought to be one who knows best the Mâzdayaçni religion; the chief of husbandmen one who takes the greatest care of his herds, and who furnishes many things for the fire; the chief of military men must be a man pure and distinguished in his qualifications of body and mind.

In a government somewhat religious, the chief of priests ought to be at the head of the chiefs of all the other professions: and such is the prerogative of the office of Dustoorân Dustoor, a dignity which is given only to *him who is most abundant in good works.* But generally, learning,

---

tively, 1, *Kâtûzyân;* 2, *Nîsâryân;* 3, *Nasûdi;* 4, *Ahnûkhûsi.* But the Vendidad and the Gathas only mention the first three classes.—*Translator.*

[45] See Vendidad, Farg. 14, paras. 6–11.—*Tr.*

[46] See Vendidad, Farg. 7, paras. 36–38.—*Tr.*

[47] See Vendidad, Farg. 18, paras. 1–6; Farg. 13, para. 45.—*Tr.*

good deeds, nobleness of sentiments, truth in words—these are what Zoroaster demands from the chiefs. He desires that they should, if possible, excel the Amshâspands themselves, who take for their model Ormazd, whom (*i. e.*, the Amshâspands) Time without Bounds[48] has clothed with his attributes.

It is particularly from the Dustoorân Dustoor that Zoroaster requires these qualifications. As he is the chief of the religion, he ought to be an example to the people; and if he sins voluntarily, the Parsis believe that he should be made to undergo, in the assembly of priests and laymen, a punishment proportionate to his crime and to his absence of temptation to commit it; for it is said in the Zend books, that *he who is without sin shall reclaim him who has committed sin ;* the Dustoor shall reclaim the layman, and the layman the Dustoor.

The authority of this sovereign Pontiff is properly spiritual. If we except some remuneration, it *now* consists only in pre-eminence of regard and outward respect, since the religion of Zoroaster has ceased to be dominant.

But when the Persian empire was in a flourishing state, the authority of this Pontiff did not extend over the priests only, of whom he was naturally the chief; but the civil usages having been connected with religious obligations, it ought to have swayed the laity, as from the time of Zoroaster, by reason of the respect and deference which the princes had for the chief of their religion.

The respect which the Parsis ought to have for the Dustoorân Dustoor and for the inferior ministers of the re-

---

[48] In refutation of this opinion of the author see p. 65, note 2. —*Translator.*

ligion is a consequence of the system of their Legislator.[49] They are obliged to respect the priests as mediators between Ormazd and his people, to maintain them and perform what they ordain when they (laymen) have sinned. The refractory are punished with death, as those who disobeyed the king were punished, from the time of Strabo, because to oppose the Minister of Ormazd is the same as to oppose Ormazd Himself.

The Parsis ought to have the same respect, the same submission to the other civil chiefs who are above them, relative to the places which they inhabit, to the states in which they live; it is this which forms the second species of jurisdiction, established by the law of Zoroaster. These chiefs are particularly kings, governors of provinces and towns, and the heads of streets and houses.[50] Each of them is respectively subordinate to him, whose rank precedes his own immediately; and the Parsis are obliged to obey them as their legitimate chiefs, whom Bahman, the angel of peace and the first of the Amshâspands next to Ormazd, has placed over society in general, and over each division of society.

This subordination does not apply to *men* alone; women are also ordained to obey the chief of their sex:[51] and the qualities of this chief ought to be such as a woman ought to possess. It is necessary that she should be of the Mâzdayaçni religion, pure, marriageable and fruitful: the models which the religion puts before this chief are Sapandomad, Ashis-Vang and Pârendi, the female angels.[52]

---

[49] Henry Lord, lib. cit. p. 189.

[50] See Vendidad, Farg. 7, paras. 41–42; Farg. 9, para. 37; Farg. 10, paras. 5–6, 9–10, &c., Méher Yasht, paras. 17–18.—*Tr.*

[51] See Yaçna, chapter 13, para. 1.—*Tr.*

[52] See Arshashang Yasht, paras. 1–22.—*Tr.*

But of all the chiefs, those on whom the Zend books expatiate most are the kings. They have a particular fire which animates them, the same which is in the presence of Ormazd; they are on the earth, what Bahman Amshâspand is in heaven. It is from Ormazd that they derive the authority which they enjoy. "*O Ormazd!*" says Zoroaster, "*Establish him king who comforts and nourishes the poor.*"

* * * * *

If the Parsi Legislator traces to God Himself the authority of kings, he prescribes to them at the same time the duties which they owe to the office they occupy. It is necessary that the chief be pure of thought, of word and of deed: Ormazd gives the empire to *him*, who comforts and nourishes the poor. *Strictness against the oppressor, and kindness towards the weak and the indigent ought to be, consequently, the essential qualities of kings.*[53]

On the other hand, the religion of Zoroaster ought to be the constant rule of their conduct, the motto for their deliberations; and as when the Persian empire existed, it was the Dustoorân Dustoor (Arch-Bishop) who explained it to the prince, one could say that the legislative power resided really in the chief of the religion. The Dâver, the chief of the Parsis, under the empire of the Mahomedans or the Hindoos, is only a feeble shadow of these ancient priestly kings.

After having regulated the general order of society by the distinction of ranks, by the necessary subordination of these ranks, and by the relations which unite the inhabitants of a place with the chief of that place, the subjects

---

[53] See Farvardin Yasht, chapter 29.—*Tr.*

with the king, Zoroaster fixes the different degrees of connections, which men ought to have between them. The number of these degrees, as well as the number of prayers which the living are obliged to have recited for the dead, depends on the distinction of ranks, which this Legislator has established as above mentioned, and is proportionate to the relations more or less near, which men have with one another.[54]

The closest connections are those of the state to its chief who represents Ormazd, and those which man contracts from his birth, viz., the reciprocal relation of the father to the son, of brothers among themselves. Afterwards, come the relationships which exist between religion and instruction; they are those which ought to be between the chiefs of Mobeds, between him who is about to be Herbed and the Herbed who instructs him, between the master and the disciple. Then comes a question of the connections which are formed by nature, but which man forms accidentally; such is the union of man and woman, which is followed, always by a proportionate diminution of degrees, by that of the just of the earth between themselves, the great of a profession, the good beings in general, the chiefs in particular:[55] and it is Mithra, the spirit who presides over the fertility of land, the Ized of good-will, the enemy of the serpent which sows envy and death—it is this Ized[56] who is charged with the creation and maintenance of this harmony among the divers races of humanity.

---

[54] See Vendidad, Fargard 12.—*Tr.*

[55] See Méher Yasht, chapter 29.—*Tr.*

[56] The other functions of Mithra are as follow :—

"Mithra or Méher Ized is represented in Zoroastrian scriptures as watching over our actions in this world, and encouraging us into, and rewarding us for, good actions, warning and punishing us for evil ones. He is the judge—Méher Dâver at the Chinvat bridge—of the

I believe it was this gradation of relationship that led Herodotus to say, that the persons, for whom the Parsis had the greatest regard, the greatest respect, were those who lived nearest to them; that they had less of it for those who lived next to these persons; thus diminishing their marks of respect in proportion as the distance increased.

Having drawn quite close the bonds of society, it was natural to insist upon the means of augmenting and enriching it, viz., population and agriculture. These objects have at all times fixed the attention of the most celebrated Legislators; Zoroaster is not content with merely recommending them to the Parsis: he makes them matters of religion; he ordains them in expiation of crimes.

The hand of the cultivator produces every good; it is the gold poniard of King Jamsheed which cleaves the earth.[57] The earth itself expresses its satisfaction[58] to man by loading him with its gifts, when after levelling it he sows seeds of herbs and trees and especially fruitful trees;[59]

---

departed souls."—See Mr. K. R. Cama's "Discourse on the Mithraic worship, &c.," p. 23.

"Mithra being the Ized of truth and light, our Dâver at the Chinvat bridge, oaths were taken and administered in his name, and hence his name was appropriately attached to the process of the passage of the sojourner through the scenes of reward and punishment of those who had followed or rejected Mithra, *i. e.*, light and truth, of those who had not or had broken Mithra, *i. e.*, an oath, or had not or had become Mithradruj by their not regarding their oaths."—*Id.* pp. 26–27.

[57] See Vendidad, Farg. 2, paras. 4–19.—*Tr.*

[58] See Vendidad, Farg. 3, paras. 3 and 23–32.—*Tr.*

[59] The Tartars of Daghestán, a country bordering on Georgia and Irán have a custom which they observe carefully, viz., that no person can marry in their tribe before having planted in a marked place 100 fruitful trees; so that one finds especially in the Mountains of Daghestán large forests of fruitful trees.—*Hist. Généolog. des Tartars*, p. 313, suite de la note a.

then he waters the land which has no water, and drains that which is inundated. The earth brings forth all sorts of fruits, when it is turned up and cultivated with care.

To sow grains with purity is to fulfil to its full extent the Mâzdayaçni law. Hence he deserves merit who thus obeys the law; the man is also great in the estimation of Ormazd, as if he had given life to a hundred, to a thousand created things, or celebrated ten thousand Yaçnas;[60] hence the obligation, when one has committed certain crimes, to give a righteous man a piece of well-irrigated ground,[61] to kill snakes which cause injury in low and marshy places, to destroy the insects which eat away the roots of trees and the seeds of grains,[62] and to build sheds to shelter men and beasts.

This last act has connection with the care of animals—the second part of the work in the fields which is not less dear to Zoroaster than the first, viz., the cultivation of lands. What pleases the earth is the multiplication and propagation of domestic animals and beasts by coupling.[63] And it is necessary to treat these animals with humanity, to nourish them,[64] to give them shelter, and finally to bestow every care, which one ought to bestow on the productions of the Good Principle, made for the benefit of the created beings of the Good Principle.

The Legislator, who recommends with so much care the cultivation of land and the multiplication of useful animals,

---

[60] See Vendidad, Farg. 3, para. 31.—*Tr.*

[61] See Vendidad, Farg. 14, para. 13.—*Tr.*

[62] See Vendidad, Farg. 14, paras. 5–6; Farg. 18, para. 73.—*Tr.*

[63] See Vendidad, Farg. 3, para. 5.—*Tr.*

[64] See Yaçna, chapter 10, para. 20; chapter 11, paras. 1–2; Vendidad, Farg. 5, para. 20.—*Tr.*

ought not to be less solicitous for the institution of marriage.[65] Herodotus and Strabo inform us that the kings of Persia made annual presents to those of their subjects who had many children. Now then, fecundity is considered equally honorable among the Parsis. They regard him a favourite of heaven, who has children of merit and in great number. Zoroaster addresses his prayer to such persons. Consequently, the day of birth is considered holy, and the Parsis celebrate it by feasts as from the time of Herodotus. It is ordained to make Daroon in the name of Hom—the Ized who gives good and pious children, the Ized who gives a sprightly and prudent husband to a long-time unmarried girl.[66] Marriage being of so great an importance, Zoroaster ought to proscribe all that can help to check or retard it. Hence, debauchery is put under the category of works which encourage the multiplication of Devs.[67] Hence, criminal intercourse with any female, whoever she may be, Parsi or foreign, is represented as one of the sources of physical and moral evil which desolates the world;[68] rape, as an irremissible crime; sodomy, as the doctrine of Devs;[69] and all these crimes are attended with capital punishment.

But it was to be feared lest the Parsis, by marrying foreigners, should lose Ormazd insensibly out of sight; or that these marriages, by transferring the wealth of families to strangers, should impoverish them. To remedy these inconveniences, to tighten the conjugal bond by a love born,

---

[65] See Vendidad, Farg. 4, paras. 44 and 47–49; Râm Yasht, chapter 10.—*Tr.*

[66] See Yaçna, chapter 9, paras. 1–23.—*Tr.*

[67] See Vendidad, Farg. 18, paras. 54–55.—*Tr.*

[68] See Vendidad, Farg. 18, paras. 61–65.—*Tr.*

[69] See Vendidad, Farg. 1, para. 12; Farg. 8, paras. 26–27, 31–32.—*Tr.*

as it were, from infancy, that is, a natural love, and to form thereby more tender and durable unions, Zoroaster recommends marriage between cousin-germans as an action meriting heaven.

Herodotus and Strabo inform us that the Parsis had many wives and concubines, and the last-named writer adds that the object was to have a great number of children. These wives and concubines probably refer to the *five species of women* whom a Parsi is permitted to marry and even to take during the life-time of his first wife, when she is barren. Except in this last case, one ought not to have at a time more than one wife: and in fact nothing more hinders multiplication than a plurality of wives.

Finally, Zoroaster takes notice of even the temper and good constitution of children. In order that they may be healthy and vigorous, he prohibits men, under the greatest punishment, from keeping company with their wives during their suckling period or their monthly course;[70] he appears to hold the same view, when prescribing the circumspection, with which females ought to be conducted to the *Armesht-gâh.*[71]

Society is established, ranks are regulated, kingdoms

---

[70] See Vendidad, Farg. 15, para. 7; Farg. 16, paras. 14–17; Farg. 18, paras. 67–76.—*Tr.*

[71] *Armesht-gâh* is a Pehlvi word, the Zend equivalent for which is *armaeshta gâtu.* It signifies "a place set apart, a spot where other men, women, children, &c., cannot go"; as for instance the place set apart for *unwell* females, the place where Mobeds undergo the *barashnûm* ceremony in the *Agiary.* *Armaeshta* in Zend originally means "still, calm, retired, undisturbed," as *armaeshta âp* meaning "still water, undisturbed or stagnant water" (see Vendidad, Farg. 6, para. 30; Aban Yasht, chap. 19; Khorshed Yasht, para. 2; Tír Yasht, chap. 11; Yaçna, chap. 68, para. 6).—*Translator.*

are formed, fields are covered with trees and cattle, mankind are increased by well-assorted marriages; it is now necessary, that a general bond should maintain that harmony, which ought to subsist between all parts of this great body. This is formed by good faith and mutual confidence, founded on verity and justice, and nourished by a spirit of moderation. This good faith renders it obligatory that what is borrowed[72] should be returned even though the lender be rich, and, consequently, in a position to give up his claim.

One is reminded in connection with this subject of what the ancients say of the manners of the Parsis. According to Herodotus, it was among them an ignominious thing to tell an untruth[73] and to incur debt: and we see, in Zenophon and Ammien-Marcellin, that their laws punished ingratitude with severity.

Zoroaster enters afterwards into the details of actions which are opposed to good faith, justice and humanity; and determines the immorality of these actions, the punishment which they deserve in proportion to the consequences they bring on society, and the degree to which distributive justice is affected.

It is a crime in general not to keep one's word, though it may not have been given on oath; it is a greater crime when one has, as it were, assured the fulfilment of a promise by an outward sign, such as putting his hand on

---

[72] See Vendidad, Farg. 4, para. 1.—*Tr.*

[73] Righteousness is the best thing for man after his birth. O Zertosht! this righteousness is the Mâzdayaçni religion; any man can purify his soul by means of good thoughts, good words and good deeds (see Vendidad, Farg. 5, para. 21; Farg. 10, para. 18).—*Translator.*

that of him whom he promises;[74] the crime is still greater, when one refuses payment of a due or salary; for instance, when one does not render what is due to the domestics and beasts, that is to say, when one does not take care of them; when one does not give to the master, who instructs him, the remuneration promised, to villages and to the people of the country, the salary which is agreed upon.

Zoroaster likewise ordains what one ought to give, according to his rank and power, to the doctor[75] who has restored him to health, or to the priest,[76] who, by purifications, has reconciled him with the Supreme Being: and if prayers are the sole reward to which the Athornâns are bound, it is because according to the system of the Persian Legislator, they have an efficacy of which the price cannot be determined.

The Parsi doctors of divinity expatiate on many of these points of morality; and, entering into the spirit of their Legislator, they prohibit, under pain of sin, the charge of compound interest on the money lent.

According to their interpretation there is not a greater crime than the buying of corn, in the expectation of selling it afterwards with profit when the market gets dear:[77] for it is said in the law, that he, who acts and accustoms himself to act in this manner, renders himself culpable for every misery, for every famine, and every distress caused in the world.

---

[74] See Vendidad, Farg. 4, paras. 2–16; Méher Yasht, paras. 2–3, 19–20, 23, 38, 82; Béherâm Yasht, para. 63.—*Tr.*

[75] See Vendidad, Farg. 7, paras. 41–43.—*Tr.*

[76] See Vendidad, Farg. 9, paras. 37–42.—*Tr.*

[77] See *Sadder Bûn-dehesh* in the old Ravâet, p. 141.

The ethics of Zoroaster goes still further. This Legislator speaks praise of him who is beneficent and liberal, of him who well supports mankind; and for greater inducement to assist the poor, he represents this action, that of giving even a few grains of corn, as accomplishing greater affliction on the Devs. The man, on the contrary, who does not give a portion of his wealth to the deserving, augments the productions of Ahriman;[78] the abode of those who do not give in charity is in hell.

Having firmly established for society the laws of distributive justice, it is expedient to prevent or check what could disturb it. Consequently, the mere thought of evil is sin; envy is represented as excited by Devs; the resolution to strike some one deserves punishment.[79] Violence is repressed by punishment proportionate to the injury inflicted on the person attacked;[80] and if Zoroaster, in the eulogy which he sings of the warriors and kings of Irán, extols their strength and courage, it is always on account of the good results to mankind which these qualities have produced, such as the destruction of the wicked and the defence of the poor and the oppressed. He exhorts, at the same time, that his heroes be humble of heart as Kaikhosru; he recommends meekness and good-nature to the people, intelligence in the good itself which they do. The man, who endeavours to increase the welfare of the people, is one of the beings to whom this Legislator addresses his prayer.

After all this, there still remains a precept of morality to be inculcated equally for the good of man and for the glory of the Good Principle, viz., to control those prompt-

---

[78] See Vendidad, Farg. 18, paras. 30–38.—*Tr.*

[79] See Vendidad, Farg. 4, paras. 18–21.—*Tr.*

[80] See Vendidad, Farg. 4, paras. 22–43.—*Tr.*

ings, which offences against us would legitimately excite; but which offences, without making amends, are a real evil to society and to our fellow-creatures, made already sufficiently unhappy by being left to go to degrading excesses. At first, man has before his eyes the example of the Master of Nature; after the Resurrection, Ormazd, touched with the repentance of sinners, will pardon them, and they shall be eternally happy with the righteous;[81] then, the Persian Legislator, by referring to what he himself does, prescribes pardon for injuries, even voluntary, and a sincere reconciliation with him from whom one has received offence. "Pardon the repenting sinner," says he, addressing Ormazd, "even if the man irritates me by his thoughts, by his "words or by his actions, carried away or not carried away "by passion, and if he humbles himself before me and "addresses his prayer, I am from that time friend of him, "who invokes me thus by Izeshné and Nyâesh."

*   *   *   *   *

Such is then the *precis* of the instructions which Zoroaster gives to the Persians in his works. This Legislator recommends, to princes and chiefs, kindness, justice and firmness; to subjects, submission and respect; to priests, purity and learning; to laymen, perfect obedience to the precepts of the religion: and this religion regards, without any distinction, all men whom it ordains to be in peace with one another, to nourish the poor, to take care of the ward, to be as good as one's word, to pay the workman, the doctor and the instructor what is their due, to plough uncultivated lands, to water them, to sink wells, to render the flocks numerous, and to kill noxious animals. We see that

---

[81] See *Sadder Bûn-dehesh* in the old Ravâet.

all these precepts tend to the good of mankind, and to the special advantage of him who conforms himself to them.

IV. The Zend and Pehlvi books present, on one side, the world created by Ormazd, and corrupted by Ahriman;[82] on the other, the re-establishment of Nature; Zoroaster appears in the field; the law which he announces contains the measures which were intended to produce this grand event.

The Parsi, instructed by this Legislator, regards himself as a soldier whom Ormazd sends under the direction of the good spirits to combat the author of evil. The prayer, which he recites after waking from sleep, puts before his mind the aim and the reward of the fights he is going to fight, the Resurrection and the glory of the saints in heaven; the water Zor, and the branches of the tree over which Hom presides, pounded in a mortar, furnish him with a juice, from which he draws his strength, while remembering the first apostle of the religion.

The girdle and a kind of shirt,[83] which mark him as the true follower of Zoroaster, are his habiliments of combat. The prayer by which he conciliates the protection of heavenly spirits; the Word which has created the world; the legal ceremonies which tend to keep the purity of his body; his absolute submission to Him from whom he has received his existence and the purity of soul—these are his arms. The precepts which he obeys render the country he inhabits fertile, cause propagation of the human race,

---

[82] In refutation of this opinion of the author see p. 66, note 3. —*Translator.*

[83] The author refers to Koshti and Sudra, outward symbols of the Zoroastrian religion.—*Translator.*

and multiplication of trees and animals, augment riches and welfare and maintain peace and public safety. Prepared for all events, he encounters evils without being beaten down by them; it would be to sin against Ormazd, and to render himself unworthy of the title of the soldier of the Good Principle, to exhibit at that time marks of excessive grief. On one side, he enjoys without scruple, but always with moderation, what Nature legitimately offers him, and believes to enter thereby in the plan of Ormazd. To deviate from this design is to augment the strength of Ahriman and to multiply his productions. * * * * Adultery, sodomy, rape, fornication, murder, violence, theft, falsehood, bad faith, voluntary infractions of the religion—these crimes are visited by punishments and sometimes by death itself. The chastisements are rigorous, because sin is the cause of evils which afflict the Parsis, of corruption which is prevalent among them; because they attack, as I have already said, the Divine Majesty, by diminishing the glory of Ormazd, and furnishing to His enemy[84] the means of overthrowing the world. But in the midst of this extreme severity, we always discover the second object of Zoroaster: he ordains punishments to secure the good of society; he wishes at the same time that Nature should enjoy her rights.

---

[84] In refutation of this opinion of the author see p. 66, note 3. —*Translator.*

A LIST OF THE BOOKS AND MANUSCRIPTS

RELATING TO

THE PARSI RELIGION,

TAKEN WITH HIM TO EUROPE

BY

MON. ANQUETIL DU PERRON.

Zend, Pehlvi and Pazend.

---

1. Zend and Pehlvi Vendidad, copied from the copy of Dustoor Jamasp.—4to, *oblong*.

2. Zend and Sanscrit Yaçna—4to.

3. Zend Vispered—4to.

4. Yashts Sádé—large 8vo.

5. A collection in three parts. The first written by Darab, containing the Khorshed Nyâesh, the Mâh Nyâesh, and the Atash Nyâesh, the Afringân Dahmân, the Afringân Gáhámbár, the prayers of Gâhs, all in Zend and Pehlvi; the original of the Pehlvi and Pazend Farhang and Hormazd Yasht in Zend and Pehlvi. The second written by Mobed Shapoor, containing the Zend and Pehlvi Vispered, Serosh Yasht in Zend, in Sanscrit and in ancient Parsi derived from Pazend, and written in Zend characters. The third containing the 9th, 10th, and 11th Hâs of Yaçna in Zend and Pazend; the Sirozâh in Zend and Pazend; the same

in Zend and Pehlvi, written by Dustoor Shapoor; the Khorshed Nyâesh (Zend and Pazend) written in Persian characters by Kika, an inhabitant of the village of Mehder, in the Paragnâh of Partchoul, situated to the east, and dependent then on Surat; and the same Nyâesh in the same languages, followed by several Nirengs and Bâjs in Gujerati, the whole written in Persian characters—8vo.

6. A collection containing (1) in Pazend (Zend characters) the Afrin Gáhámbár, the Nâm Setâeshné, the Afrin Zartosht; (2) in Zend, the Ardibéhésht Yasht and the Venant Yasht; (3) in Pazend (Zend characters) a portion of the Ravâet, which treats, among other things, of the Atash Behrám, of King Jamsheed and of the origin of the Gáhámbárs, &c.; (4) in Pazend (Persian characters) the *Eulma Eslam* and two prefaces to the Sháh Námeh—4to.

7. A small Ravâet which contains the Sirozâh in Zend; some details on the ceremonies and practices of the Zoroastrian religion, some prayers, &c.—all mixed up in Zend and Pazend, followed by several letters of the Dustoors of Kirmán and of India, relative to the religion, among which is one treating of the *Nowroz*—12mo.

Persian.

1. Farhang-e Jehangiri—An excellent Persian Dictionary, finished in the reign of Jehangir—folio.

2. Bourân-e Kâté—A comprehensive and accurate Persian Dictionary, compiled by Mohamed Hossein who flou-

rished in 1651 A. C.—folio, ruled, perfectly well-written; the only copy in Europe, copied at Surat, in 1730 A. C.

3. An epitome of Farhang-e Serouri—A dictionary in five parts, of which the fourth contains some words said to have been derived from Zend and Pazend.

4. Sadder—A treatise in verse on the moral and ceremonial theology of the Parsis—8vo.

5. Mino-Khéred, in verse—12mo.

6. Sháh-Námeh—A Poem of sixty-four thousand verses, composed at the end of the tenth century by Firdosi Tusy, comprising the history of the Parsis from Gayomard to Yezdegird, their last king of the Sassanian dynasty in the seventh century after Christ —folio, with illustrations.

7. Kérshasp Námeh—A history in verse of Kérshasp and many other Iranian heroes of the time of Zohâk and the first kings of the Kyânian dynasty—8vo.

8. Barzo Námeh—A Persian poem of more than sixty thousand verses, composed by Atai, a celebrated poet, but inferior to Firdosi. It contains the history of Rustom, Sohráb, Barzo, &c.—2 vols. with illustrations, the only copy in Europe.

9. A precious collection containing the Farâmarz Námeh, the Jehangir Námeh and the Bânoo Gushasp Námeh, that is to say, the history of Farâmarz, Jehangir (son of Rustom) and Bânoo Gushasp (daughter of Rustom) —8vo.

10. A collection containing the Zertosht Námeh, preceded by the history of the Retreat of the Parsis in India —12mo.

11. A collection containing the Changraghâch Námeh and the Jâmâspi, in verse—8vo.

12. Bahman Námeh—A history in verse of Bahman (son of Aspandiâr, son of Gushtasp, a king of the Kyânian dynasty) composed at the end of the eleventh century—4to.

13. Darab Námeh—A work containing an account of the last years of Bahman, son of Aspandiâr, a part of the lives of Homâi, Darab, the last Darab, and a fragment of the expeditions of Alexander—folio, copied in 1584 A. C.

14. A collection containing the history in verse of the *amours* of Azâd Bakht, king of Persia, of Firooz Bakht, king of Egypt and of Ershad, son of the king of Katay—12mo.

Virâf Námeh (in Gujerati)—4to, with illustrations.*

---

* Besides these, the French author carried with him to Europe 93 other Mss. as follow :—66 Mss. in Persian ; 7, in Arabic ; 2, in Turkish ; 3, in Moorish (in Persian characters) ; 2, in Gujerati ; 6, in Sanscrit ; 6, in Tamil and 1, in Canarese.—*Translator.*

BOOKS WHICH MONS. ANQUETIL DU PERRON COULD NOT OBTAIN.

---

1. The Nyâeshs of Fire, the Moon and the Sun, in Sanscrit.*

2. The Nyâeshs of Water and Mithra, in Pehlvi and Sanscrit.

3. The Hormazd Yasht in Sanscrit.

4. The Târif Sirozâh in Pehlvi, from the 17th day to the 30th. This book, it was believed, was to be found entire in the hands of the sons of Bahmanji Shett.†

5. The Pehlvi Yaçna.

6. The Nirengastán—A work in 4to from 20 to 25 *cahiers* treating principally of the ceremonies of the Parsi religion, in the commencement whereof is described the *Vars.*

7. The first six Fargards of the Vendidad in Sanscrit.

8. The Gushtasp Yasht, brought from Kirmán (according to what the Parsis of Surat say) 400 years ago by Méhriâr Marzbân ; the Sâm Námeh, the Taimoor Námeh, and the Farâmarz Námeh.

---

* I was told that this book could be had at Nowsaree.—*Anquetil du Perron.*

† Afterwards I was assured that they had not got it.—*Anquetil du Perron.*

APPENDIX.

☞ *Extracts from Dr. M. Haug's "Essays on the sacred language, writings and religion of the Parsis" in support of the Zoroastrian doctrine that the First Cause which created the whole universe is Ahuramazda (the name of God throughout the Zend-Avesta) and not Zarvâna Akarana.*

The real doctrines of Zarathustra, untouched by the speculations of later ages, can be learnt only from the old Yaçna, chiefly from the Gâthas. The leading idea of his theology was *Monotheism, i. e.*, that there are not many gods, but only one, and the principle of his speculative philosophy *Dualism, i. e.*, the supposition of two primeval causes of the real world and of the intellectual, while his moral philosophy was moving in the *Triad* of thought, word and deed. His predecessors, the Soshyanto, seem to have been worshipping a plurality of good spirits, whom they called *Ahuras, i. e.*, the living ones who were opposed to the Devas. Spitama, not satisfied with this indistinct expression of the Divine Being, reduced this plurality to an unity. The new name, by which he called the Supreme Being, was *Ahurô Mazdâo* which means "the living Creator of the universe"......In the Sassanian times the name was changed to *Ahurmazd*, and in modern Persian to *Hormazd* or *Ormazd* which form is used by the Parsis now-a-days.

Zarathustra Spitama's conception of Ahuramazda as the Supreme Being is perfectly identical with the notion of *Elohîm* or *Jehovah*, which we find in the books of the Old Testament. Ahuramazda is called by him "the Creator of the earthly and spiritual life, the Lord of the whole universe at whose hands are all the creatures." He is the light and the source of light; he is the wisdom and intellect. He is in possession of all good things, spiritual and worldly, such as the good mind *(vohu manô)*, immortality *(ameretât)*, wholesomeness *(haurvatât)*, the best truth *(asha vahista)*, devotion and piety (*ârmaiti*), and abundance of every earthly good* *(khshathra vairya)*. All these gifts he grants to the righteous pious man, who is pure in thoughts, words and deeds. But he, as the ruler of the whole universe, does not only reward the good, but he is a punisher of the wicked at the same time (see Yaçna 45, 5). All that is created good or evil, fortune or misfortune, is his work (see Yaçna 48, 4; 51, 6). A separate evil spirit of equal power with Ahuramazda, and always opposed to him is entirely strange to Zarathustra's theology, though the existence of such an opinion among the ancient Zoroastrians can be gathered from some later books.

The opinion, so generally believed now, that Zarathustra was preaching Dualism, that is to say, the supposition of two original independent spirits, a good and a bad one, utterly distinct from each other, and one counteracting the creation of the other, is owing to a confusion of his philosophy with his theology. Having arrived at the grand idea of the unity, and indivisibility of the Supreme Being, he undertook to solve the great problem, on which so many a wise man of antiquity and even of modern times was engaged, viz., how are the imperfections discoverable in the world, the various kinds of evils, wickedness and baseness, compatible with the goodness, holiness and justice of God? The great thinker of so remote an antiquity solved the difficult question *philosophically* by the supposition of two primeval causes, which, though different, were united, and produced the world of the material things, as well as that of the spirit, which doctrine may best be learnt from Yaçna 30.

The two primeval principles are *Spentô mainyus* and *Angrô mainyus*; these spirits are united in one and the same being, viz., Ahuramazda, and represent only both sides of the divine nature, the creative and life-giving, as well as the destructive and life-taking powers. That *Angrô mainyus* is no separate being opposed to Ahuramazda, is

* See chiefly Yaçna 47, 1.

unmistakeably to be gathered from Yaçna 19, 9, where Ahuramazda is mentioning his "two spirits," who are inherent to his own nature, and in other passages (Yaçna 57) distinctly called the "two Creators" "the two masters" *(pâyû)*. And, indeed, we never find mentioned in the Gâthas, Angrô mainyus as a constant opponent to Ahuramazda as is the case in later writings. Spentô mainyus was regarded as the author of all that is bright and shining, of all that is good and useful in nature, while Angrô mainyus called into existence all that is dark, and apparently noxious. Both are inseparable, as day and night, and though opposed to each other, are indispensable for the preservation of creation......Life is produced by Spentô mainyus, but extinguished by Angrô mainyus.

Such is the original Zoroastrian notion of the two creative spirits, who form only two sides of the Divine Being. But in the course of time, this doctrine of the great founder was, in consequence of misunderstandings, and false interpretations, changed and corrupted. Spentô mainyus was taken as a name of Ahuramazda himself; then, of course Angrô mainyus, by becoming entirely separated from Ahuramazda, was regarded as the constant adversary of Ahuramazda, and thus the Dualism, God and Devil, was called forth. Either was an independent ruler, one endeavouring to destroy the creation of the other, and thus both waging constantly war......In consequence of this entire separation of the two sides of Ahuramazda and the substitution of two independent rulers, governing the universe, the unity and oneness of the Supreme Being was lost, Monotheism was superceded by Dualism. But this deviation from, and entire change of, the prophet's doctrine could not satisfy the minds of all the divines and philosophers in ancient Persia. It very likely was only the innovation of an influential party or sect, probably that one which is called *Zendik, i. e.*, followers of the interpretation (Zend), and which was opposed by that of the *Magi*.* That Dua-

* The Magi were chiefly spread in the West, in Media and Persia; the Zendiks in the East, in Bactria. The former seem to have acknowledged only the Avesta or original texts of the sacred writings; the latter followed the traditional explanation, called Zend.

lism was actually the doctrine of the Zendiks, we best learn from the commencement of the Bundehesh, which book purports to expound the lore of this party. The Magi seem still to have clung to the prophet's doctrine of the Oneness of the Supreme Being. But to refute the heretical opinions of the Zendiks, which were founded on interpretations of passages from the sacred texts, a new and fresh proof of the Unity of the Supreme Being was required. This was found in the term "*Zarvâna akarana*," *i. e.*, time without bounds, which we meet occasionally in the Zend Avesta. The chief passage, no doubt, was Vend. 19, 9; but the interpretation for proving that *Zarvâna akarana* means the Supreme Being, out of whom Ahuramazda and Angrô mainyus are said to have sprung up, rests on a grammatical misunderstanding of the words *Zruni akaranê.* Anquetil, according to the teaching of his masters, the Dustoors, translates them as nominative case, whilst a very superficial knowledge of Zend and Sanscrit grammars suffices to recognise both the forms as so called locatives: they are therefore to be translated only "in the boundless time," the subject of the sentence being *Spentô mainyus*, *i. e.*, the white spirit (a name of Ormazd); were it the nominative case, and the subject of the sentence, then we should have to expect "*Zàrva akaranem.*" The right translation is as follows:—

"Oh evil-knowing Angrô mainyus (Ahriman)! *Ahuramazda* made these good weapons *in the boundless time*, the immortal holy Saints, the rulers and masters of the good creation, assisted Him in *making them.*"

The true meaning of the expression, that "Ahuramazda created in the boundless time," is, that God (Ahuramazda) is from eternity, self-existing, neither born nor created. Only an eternal being can be independent of the bounds of time to which all mortals are subject.